Enchanting HORSES

Enchanting HORSES

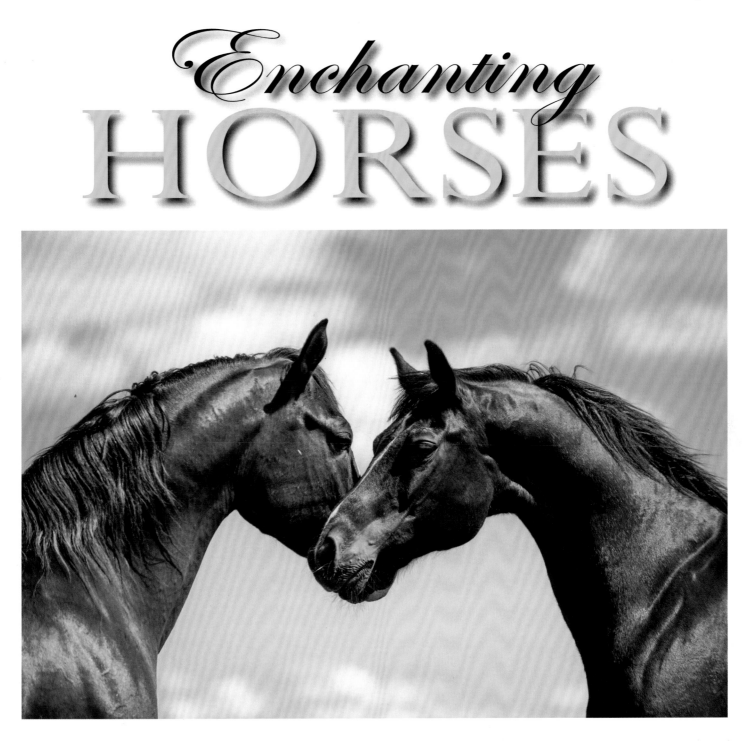

Jennifer Anderson

METRO BOOKS

NEW YORK

METRO BOOKS
New York

An Imprint of Sterling Publishing Co., Inc.
1166 Avenue of the Americas
New York, NY 10036

Distributed in Canada
by Sterling Publishing Co., Inc.
c/o Canadian Manda Group, 664 Annette Street,
Toronto, Ontario, Canada M6S 2C8

For information about custom editions, special
sales, and premium and corporate purchases, please
contact Sterling Special Sales at 800-805-5489 or
specialsales@sterlingpublishing.com.

Manufactured in China

2 4 6 8 10 9 7 5 3 1

www.sterlingpublishing.com

CONTENTS

Oh, a wonderful horse is the Fly-Away Horse -
Perhaps you have seen him before;
Perhaps, while you slept, his shadow has swept

Through the moonlight that floats on the floor.
For it's only at night, when the stars twinkle bright,
That the Fly-Away Horse, with a neigh
And a pull at his rein and a toss of his mane,
Is up on his heels and away!
The Moon in the sky,
As he gallopeth by,
Cries: "Oh! what a marvelous sight!"
And the Stars in dismay
Hide their faces away
In the lap of old Grandmother Night.

It is yonder, out yonder, the Fly-Away Horse
Speedeth ever and ever away -
Over meadows and lanes, over mountains and plains,
Over streamlets that sing at their play;
And over the sea like a ghost sweepeth he,
While the ships they go sailing below,
And he speedeth so fast that the men at the mast
Adjudge him some portent of woe.
"What ho there!" they cry,
As he flourishes by
With a whisk of his beautiful tail;
And the fish in the sea
Are as scared as can be,
From the nautilus up to the whale!

And the Fly-Away Horse seeks those faraway lands
You little folk dream of at night -
Where candy-trees grow, and honey-brooks flow,
And corn-fields with popcorn are white;
And the beasts in the wood are ever so good
To children who visit them there -
What glory astride of a lion to ride,
Or to wrestle around with a bear!
The monkeys, they say:
"Come on, let us play,"
And they frisk in the cocoanut-trees:
While the parrots, that cling
To the peanut-vines, sing
Or converse with comparative ease!

Off! scamper to bed - you shall ride him tonight!
For, as soon as you've fallen asleep,
With a jubilant neigh he shall bear you away
Over forest and hillside and deep!
But tell us, my dear, all you see and you hear
In those beautiful lands over there,
Where the Fly-Away Horse wings his faraway course
With the wee one consigned to his care.
Then grandma will cry
In amazement: "Oh, my!"
And she'll think it could never be so;
And only we two
Shall know it is true -
You and I, little precious! shall know!

~ "The Fly-Away Horse" by Eugene Field

CHAPTER ONE
THE ORIGINS OF
THE HORSE

"There is something about the outside of a horse that is good for the inside of a man."

—Winston Churchill

It has taken nearly 60 million years for the horse to evolve from its earliest form, *Hyrocotherium* or *Eohippus*, to *Equus caballus* of the family *Equidae*, the modern horse as we know it today.

Eohippus (Dawnhorse) can be traced back to the Eocene period, between 56 and 34 million years ago, and it is thought to have originated in Africa or Asia. Fossils indicate that it was the size of a small dog and weighed about 12 pounds (5.5 kilograms); instead of having one toe protected by a hoof, as in the modern horse, it had paw pads, with four toes on the front feet and three on the back.

Eohippus was a forest dweller, where it grazed among low-growing shrubs and tender leaves. Perfectly suited to its environment, its light-brown dappled coat provided excellent camouflage and making it almost invisible to predators.

ABOVE: *The Asiatic Horse or Przewalski's horse (*Equus caballus przewalskii*) was discovered in Mongolia by the explorer Nicolai Przewalski in the late 19th century.*

LEFT: *A cave painting at Lascaux in the Dordogne, France, clearly shows a horse-like creature. It was painted around 15000 BC.*

OPPOSITE: *The Konik is thought to be a distant relative of the now extinct Tarpan horse.*

ABOVE: The Somali Wild Ass is a subspecies of the African Wild Ass. It is found in Somalia, the southern Red Sea region of Eritrea, and the Afar Region of Ethiopia. It has the dorsal and zebra stripes of a primitive species.

RIGHT: The Exmoor is descended from the Celtic or Plateau pony. There are still herds living wild up on the moors in Exmoor National Park, Devon, England.

During the Oligocene period, which began 34 million years ago, *Eohippus* evolved into *Mesohippus* and *Miohippus*. While still forest browsers, these were larger, taller and heavier animals. Their teeth had changed from small and sharp to larger and blunter, and therefore their diet evolved. The feet had also changed: there were now three toes on the front feet, the middle one bearing most of the body's weight.

The major evolutionary leap came in the Miocene period, 24 million years ago, when climatic change transformed once swampy forests into great plains.

Parahippus and eventually Merychippus now stood firmly on a single toe but still retained the side toes. They were larger than their predecessors with longer legs which, because they could no longer rely on the cover of trees, enabled them to flee from predators. Like other animals adapted to open spaces, eyes were positioned to the sides of skulls, allowing them to scan distances and spot predators more readily.

ABOVE & OPPOSITE: The Dutch Heavy Draft (above) and the Brabant (opposite) are two of many heavy, coldblooded European breeds, probably descended from Equus caballus sylvaticus, or the Forest Horse.

The next significant development came around 10 million years ago, when the first horses appeared standing firmly on one toe. By now, the side toes had atrophied to what are known as splint bones, situated further up the leg. Now known as *Pliohippus*, this was very much more like *Equus* as we know it today, adapted for cropping grass and for running fast, though still smaller and lighter than the modern horse.

The horse made its final leap to *Equus* during the Pleistocene period, about 2 million years ago. By now it was perfectly adapted to life on the plains. It was strong, fast and well-muscled and so prolific that it quickly spread throughout Asia and Europe and across the Bering Strait into America.

PRIMITIVE HORSES: THE THREE BASIC TYPES

It is thought that among the primitive horses of Eurasia there were three types, depending upon their habitat and the region in which they lived. The scientific classification given to these horses is *Equus caballus*, which is also the name of the modern horse.

Of the three types, the Forest Horse (*Equus caballus sylvaticus*) was the heaviest in stature and is probably the ancestor of the heavier breeds known throughout Europe. It was ideally suited to the wet marshlands of Europe, where its thick coat protected it against all weather and particularly harsh winters.

The Asiatic Horse (*Equus caballus przewalskii*) was discovered in Mongolia by Nicolai Przewalski around 1881.

It is small and tough and capable of surviving harsh conditions. While it is considered an important ancestor of the modern horse, it is distinguished by a slightly different genetic make-up. Although no longer found in the wild, it is still bred in zoos and safari parks.

The third type, the Tarpan (*Equus caballus gomelini*), evolved on the steppes of eastern Europe and western Asia. Well-suited to life on open plains, the Tarpan had a lighter build and was faster than the other two types but like them was capable of withstanding extreme climatic conditions.

DOMESTICATION

The first horses were domesticated in eastern Europe and the Near East about 5,000 years ago. At that time, other animals, such as goats, sheep, cows, and dogs had been already successfully domesticated, but it was the need for a larger beast of burden, and one that would produce milk and meat, which led to the domestication of the horse. It was not until later that horses would be used for riding. By 1000 BC, domesticated horses could be found all over Europe, Asia, and North Africa. From the original three

ABOVE: The Icelandic Horse is descended from Pony Type 1. It is small and sturdy, and bred to withstand the harsh climate of northern Europe.

OPPOSITE: The Fjord pony with its dorsal stripe is descended from Pony type 2. Like Pony Type 1 it is also aclimatized to a cold and harsh environment.

types of primeval horse, four types of domesticated horses emerged, two of which could be classified as ponies and two of which are classified as horses.

Pony Type 1 stood around 12hh (hands high) tall and inhabited north-western Europe. It would have looked very similar to the Shetland Pony we know today, with a small sturdy body and thick coat. It would also have been perfectly acclimatized to the conditions of its habitat. Also known as the Celtic or Plateau Pony, breeds such as the Exmoor and Icelandic descended from it, producing the relatively small, chunky breeds we know today.

Pony Type 2 was somewhat larger, standing about 14.1hh. It evolved in Eurasia and as a result became extremely

OPPOSITE: The striking Akhal-Teke displays the characteristics of horses which descend from Horse Type 1.

ABOVE: The Barb is ancient breed which is thought to date back to 8th-century North Africa. Accustomed to desert conditions it is also descended from Horse Type 1.

hardy and resistant to the cold climatic conditions of the region. It was usually dun in color and had a dorsal stripe along its back and stripes on the legs. Prezewalski, Norwegian and Fjord ponies are all descendants of Pony Type 2.

Horse Type 1 was larger than the first two, standing at 14.3hh, and had become adapted to the deserts and steppes of Europe and central Asia. It could withstand long periods of drought and heat and as a result had a fine coat and a relatively thin skin. It had a longish head, long neck and

sparse tail and mane. It is a close relative of the old Turkmene horse and also of today's Akhal-Teke. Its bloodline has also found its way into the modern Andalusian and Barb.

Horse Type 2, like type 1, was predominantly a desert horse but rather smaller at 12hh. Its home was western Asia and it was hardy and could withstand extreme weather. A horse of great beauty with a fine head and body, this is the forefather of today's Arabian.

ABOVE & OPPOSITE: The Arabian horse originated in the Arabian Peninsula. With a distinctive head shape and high tail carriage, the Arabian is one of the most easily recognizable horse breeds in the world. Being a desert horse it can withstand extreme heat and has enormous stamina. It is a descendant of Horse Type 2.

THE FIRST RIDDEN HORSES

The earliest records describing horses used for riding originated in Persia (Iran) and date from the third millennium BC. By 1580 BC, horses were also ridden in Egypt, and later in Greece. This was a departure from previous uses. Horses had been regarded as beasts of burden and riding them was of secondary importance. Throughout the centuries, moreover, horse riding began almost to assume the status of an art form. Xenophon (ca. 435–354 BC), a historian and military leader famous for leading the retreat of 10,000 mercenaries for 900 miles (1500km), helped change the status by founding equestrianism in Athens: his definitive book on the subject is still highly regarded today.

Increasingly, riding horses came to be used for other purposes, as warhorses or for pulling chariots, tasks for which they had no rivals for centuries. Horses also played an important part in agriculture until they were replaced by steam traction and the internal combustion engine.

ABOVE: Today horseback riding is largely for sport and recreation.

RIGHT: The Thoroughbred is the result of selective breeding over centuries. It is bred for the speed and stamina required for racing.

CHAPTER TWO
EQUINE BREEDS & TYPES

"All you need for happiness is a good gun, a good horse, and a good wife."

—Daniel Boone

Horses and ponies belong to one of two specific groups: breeds and types. A breed consists of horses and ponies which are genetically similar and which have been selectively bred to produce consistent characteristics, while reinforcing their best features; they are recognized as such in official stud books. They fall into four distinct categories: hotbloods, warmbloods, coldbloods, and ponies.

LEFT: Warmbloods are the product of regional coldblooded horses, bred with hotbloods such as Arabs and Thoroughbreds. They excel in dressage, showjumping, and eventing.

ABOVE: The Hunter is classified as a type in that it has been bred for a specific purpose.

OPPOSITE: Ponies are suitable to be ridden, driven, or kept as pets.

Hotbloods are highly strung and include Thoroughbreds and Arabs. They have been bred for their enormous stamina and speed, evident when racing, in which they excel.

Warmbloods are calmer creatures, having a heavier build than hotbloods. They have been bred for their extravagant paces and biddable natures, making them excellent performers at jumping and dressage. They are the result of interbreeding with heavier coldbloods such as Shires and Cleveland Bays and were originally bred as warhorses and for lighter work on farms, mainly in northern Europe. Examples are the Hanoverian, Dutch Warmblood, and Holstein.

Coldbloods, as mentioned above, are heavier types of horses such as Irish Drafts and Percherons. They are less common nowadays, heavy horses on farms being a thing of the past, and are now more often seen in the show ring.

Finally, there is the pony, which covers all the native breeds measuring less than 14.2hh.

A type, however, is the result of crossing breeds to produce a specific kind of horse intended for a specific purpose, such as the cob and the hunter.

LEFT: The Shire is a breed developed for its incredible strength. It is suitable for pulling heavy loads.

CHAPTER THREE
COLORS

"The horse is God's gift to mankind."

—Arabian Proverb

The wild horses that originally roamed the world would have been a dull muddy color, allowing them to blend in with their surroundings. Nowadays, through selective breeding, horses come in a variety of colors and markings.

Breeding horses to produce certain colors is a complicated business and is achieved by mixing various genetic material. This is a tricky process as some color genes also have an effect on temperament and performance. For example, the old saying that chestnuts have a fiery temperament often seems correct. Racehorse breeders tend to favor horses carrying the black gene, present in the bay, and they do seem predominant among the winners.

In the United States and Australia, particularly, selective breeding to produce unusual colors has become

LEFT: The Konik, a descendent of the now extinct Tarpan, displays the typical muddy coloring and dorsal stripe of its ancient ancestors.

ABOVE: The Paint Horse has been selectively bred for its striking markings and color combinations.

OPPOSITE: Left to right: a roan, a chestnut, and a palomino.

commonplace, and horses now come in a striking variety of colors and markings. However, most horses fit into the basic categories listed in this section.

BAY

This is probably the most common color, the coat varying from a light reddish-brown to deep black-brown with black on the lower legs, muzzle and the tips of the ears, the mane and tail being also black. Bays are a genetically modified form of black. Despite its popularity, only one actual breed has emerged: the Cleveland Bay.

ABOVE: The coat of the dark bay can vary from a rich-brown to almost black.

OPPOSITE: The bright bay has a striking, reddish coat, and a black mane and tail.

BROWN

The coat consists of shades of nearly black or brown, which are spread evenly over the body except for the areas around the eyes, the girth, muzzle, and flanks, which have a lighter "mealy" appearance. The mane and tail may be liver, reddish-brown, or nearly black.

ABOVE: A brown mare with her bay foal.

OPPOSITE: The coat of a brown horse differs from the bay because it is invariably chocolate in color. It tends not to have any redness to it.

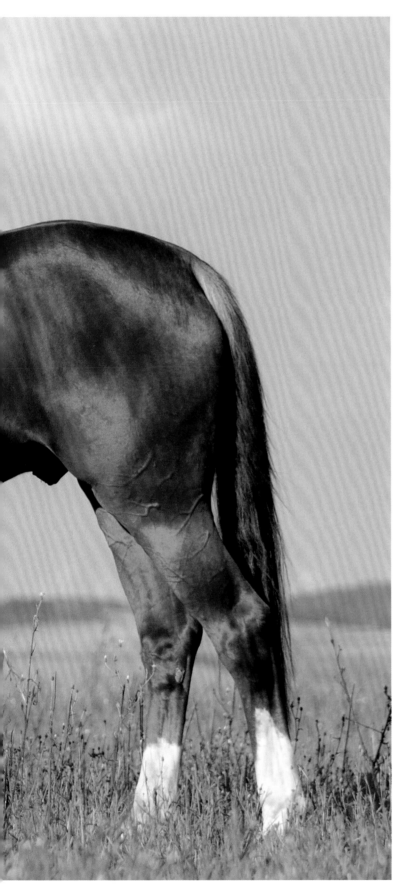

CHESTNUT

This is a red coat of any shade, ranging from a light to a dark reddish-brown which is known as liver chestnut. The mane and tail are usually of a similar color or may be flaxen (these are called sorrels). Non-chestnut parents may have chestnut foals; if both parents are chestnut they will always have progeny that are this color.

LEFT: Brightly colored chestnuts like this one are often associated with a fiery temperment.

ABOVE: A liver chestnut.

DUN

There are four variations on the color known as dun, which can have red, yellow, mouse and blue tinges. Dun horses have darker markings on the muzzle and legs with the addition of a dorsal stripe which may be black or brown. Several breeds of this color type have been developed, the most common being the Fjord.

ABOVE & OPPOSITE: There has been a resurgence in popularity for the dun, with many breeds now appearing in this color. Below is a dun Quarter Horse and to the right is a dun Lusitano. Very similar to the dun is the buckskin which is also very popular. It has a lighter shade of mane and tail when compared to the dun and lacks a dorsal stripe.

GRAY

Technically, this is not a color but a pattern superimposed over other colors. Grays are born with dark skin which progressively lightens with age, leading to most of them eventually turning white in varying degrees. This is not necessarily a sign of old age and is known as graying out. They come with two different coat patterns, the favorite being dappled gray, which is usually the result of the lightening of the coat of a horse which was born dark gray, known as iron or blue-gray. As the horse's color fades, the dappling remains mainly on the legs. The other type is known as flea-bitten; these grays never turn completely white, but seem to revert instead to the base color they had at birth: for example, some may develop blue, black, or red speckles; moreover, injuries such as bites and cuts will also grow over in that color.

BELOW: This young horse is a dapple gray. As a gray gets older, its coat will usually fade to a lighter shade.

OPPOSITE: The top photograph is of an iron gray, below left is a gray that has faded to white and below right is a flea-bitten gray.

BLACK

There are two types: non-fading black, which only fades under extreme conditions, the overall effect being a coat of a metallic, iridescent, or bluish shine. When combined with white markings, such as stars or socks, it is particularly striking. Fading black is probably a more common

BELOW: This horse has a black coat which will usually fade as summer progresses. Its coat already has a reddish sheen caused by sunlight and sweat.

OPPOSITE: This Friesian has an inky black coat which is so dense in color it is less likely to fade.

variation: the black color will only be retained if the horse is kept stabled or rugged when exposed to the elements. There may also be fading through sweating, when lighter patches occur under the saddle and girth areas. When the summer coat comes through, the coat will have a black sheen, but never the blue metallic effect of the non-fading type, and during the season will become a reddish-brown in appearance. Black horses aren't popular where the climate is hot, such as the Australian outback, as black absorbs heat, leading to skin irritation. Breeds selectively bred for their black color tend to appear in colder climates, for example, in the Fell and Friesian.

SPOTTED

Spotting can occur in many breeds but is most common in the Appaloosa; in fact, the breed has given its name to the spotted pattern. Markings vary from colored spots on white, white spots on a base color, or a scattering of small white or colored spots.

LEFT: The Appaloosa comes in many variations of colors and patterns.

ABOVE: The Knabstrupper tends to have more uniform spots.

PALOMINO

Much prized, these horses have beautiful golden coats ranging from pale to dusky tan; they are usually the result of a cremello crossed with a chestnut. However, the breeding of palominos is a complicated business and is more common in the United States where the color originated. Ideally, the mane and tail should be pure white.

ABOVE & OPPOSITE: The palomino is famous for its beautiful looks. While the shade of theirs coat may vary, all palominos have striking white manes and tails.

CREMELLO

Sometimes known as pseudo-albinos, these horses have cream-colored coats which are slightly darker then any

OPPOSITE & BELOW: The cremello is strikingly beautiful. In sunnier countries it requires extra protection from sunlight.

white markings present. The eyes are pale blue and glassy in appearance. This color is not popular, particularly in hot climates, where strong sunlight can irritate light-colored eyes. Such horses are also more prone to skin cancers and chafing. However, in cooler climates they can do rather better and their striking appearance is certainly unusual.

OPPOSITE: A strawberry roan is predominantly chestnut with white hairs throughout its coat.

ABOVE: This Quarter Horse is a blue roan.

RIGHT: The bay roan is predominantly bay with white hairs throughout its coat.

ROAN

This comes in a variety of colors and is composed of a pattern of white hairs over a base color which is only confined to the body, the head and legs remaining in the base color. Unlike grays, the color does not fade, but any nicks or scratches will grow back covered in the base color. They come in three basic types: strawberry roan, which has a chestnut base coat, blue roan which has black, and red roan which has bay. The mane, tail, legs, and muzzle markings will be the same color as the base coat.

COLORED

The definition of a colored horse is any color combined with white. In the United States, these are known as pintos or paint; however, there is a huge variety of colors and markings with varying degrees of white and color which have different names. They are highly prized and their appearance is extremely striking. In Britain, colored types are less popular and tend to be predominately ponies: however, horses of the type are now becoming more common. Varieties are skewbald, which are coats with any color patches with white, and piebald, which is black-and-white.

BELOW: This colored mare is an unusal combination bay roan, black, white, and brown. Her foal is a chestnut skewbald.

OPPOSITE: The striking markings of a handsome piebald.

CHAPTER FOUR
HORSES LIVING WILD

"The horses paw and prance and neigh,
Fillies and colts like kittens play,
And dance and toss their rippled manes
Shining and soft as silken skeins…"

—Oliver Wendell Holmes

Mankind's encounters with horses, throughout much of history, have been with the domesticated kind, for the horse has lived side by side with us for thousands of years. Once used as warhorses, as beasts of burden and for transporting human beings, the horse's modern-day purpose seems to be solely for our pleasure, which is a far cry from its true evolution as a wild, free-roaming herd animal.

Naturally gregarious and highly social, horses are at their happiest with others of their kind, surrounded by

OPPOSITE: Reminiscent of the American Mustang, the Australian Brumby, belongs to the largest group of horses in the world that live in a wild state.

ABOVE: The Camargue is an ancient indigenous breed which inhabits the wetlands region of the Rhône Delta in the south of France.

RIGHT: The Dartmoor is one of the U.K.'s native breeds that grazes on the moors of Dartmoor National Park, Devon, England.

OVERLEAF: Domesticated horses allowed to live in the wild will display similar characteristics of true wild horses.

plenty of open space, so it is hardly surprising that once freedom is allowed they should revert to natural behavior. In the wild, horses form themselves into a herd, with a dominant stallion as their leader, which protects its group of mares and youngsters. The herd forms a close unit, its members playing, grooming, feeding, and resting together,

all the while keeping a watchful eye for signs of danger. During the mating season, the stallion will fight for herd dominance, securing for itself plenty of breeding females in the process.

Horses have evolved to be perfectly adapted to living in the open. They are powerful sprinters capable of achieving significant speeds when fleeing from danger. They have large eyes, set on the sides of their heads, which provide almost all-round vision. They also have extremely good hearing, and their mobile, pointed ears allow them to catch sounds from all angles.

The instinct to heard provides the group with relative safety compared with that of a lone animal; a galloping group tends to confuse would-be predators, while any animal that is brought down would more likely be one that is weak or sick.

The term "wild horse" is also used colloquially to refer to free-roaming herds of feral horses such as the Mustang in the United States, the Brumby in Australia, and many others. These feral horses are untamed members of the domestic horse subspecies (*Equus ferus caballus*) and should not be confused with the two truly "wild" horse subspecies, the Tarpan or Eurasian Wild Horse (*Equus ferus ferus*), once native to Europe and western Asia, and Przewalski's Horse (*Equus ferus przewalskii*).

LEFT: A herd of Mustangs in the Nevada Desert, Nevada, U.S.A.

OVERLEAF: Wild horses in the National Park Torres del Paine, Patagonia, Chile.

CHAPTER FIVE
HORSES OF THE AMERICAS

"I bless the hoss from hoof to head -
From head to hoof, and tale to mane! -
I bless the hoss, as I have said,
From head to hoof, and back again!"

—James Whitcomb Riley

AMERICAN MINIATURE HORSE

This is not a pony but a scaled-down version of a horse; consequently it has all the characteristics of the larger animal. The first true miniature horses appeared in Europe in the 1600s, where they were bred as pampered pets for the nobility. Unfortunately, not all miniatures had such a good life and many were used as pit ponies in the coal mines of northern Europe, including the English Midlands. In the

OPPOSITE, ABOVE & OVERLEAF: The Miniature horse is friendly and sociable, and for this reason it is often kept as a family pet. It is a sweet-natured, intelligent, and quick learning breed that can be long-lived. They make excellent all-rounders and excel in showjumping and showing.

1900s Lady Estella Hope continued the breeding program, and these are the lines that probably made their way to the United States.

Today the American Miniature Horse is stylish, well-proportioned and the product of nearly 400 years of selective breeding. They make excellent all-rounders, especially in children's ridden classes such as showjumping and showing, and are also used for driving. The breed now has a closed stud book managed by the American Miniature Horse Association.

The American Miniature Horse should not exceed 34 inches (86cm) or 9hh. It should have a similar conformation

to a large, fine-boned horse such as a Thoroughbred or Warmblood. The overall impression should be of well-balanced symmetry, accompanied by strength, agility, and alertness; essentially, it should have all the appearance of the perfect horse in miniature.

The horse has a kind and affectionate nature. It is also gentle and placid, making it an ideal companion animal. It is excellent for children, and inspires confidence because it is easy to mount and willing to be ridden; its small stature also makes it suitable for the less physically able. The foals are particularly attractive, ranging from 16–21 inches (41–53cm) in height. They can be all colors and achieve no more than 9hh in height.

AMERICAN SADDLEBRED

The American Saddlebred was developed from horses originally brought to America from Europe in the 1600s, and particularly from Britain and what is now the Irish Republic. They had been used for trotting and pacing, and their hardy constitutions and extravagant paces made them popular in their new home.

The Narragansett Pacer, which was developed in Rhode Island in the 17th century, is believed to have been an ancestor of these European horses, and it was the model on which all easy-gaited horses in America were based thereafter.

Now extinct, the Pacer was noted for its docility and easy motion, making long days in the saddle more comfortable for the rider in the early days of the American colonies. Narragansett mares and Thoroughbred stallions were allowed to mate, with the result that the pacing gait and

all-round ability were transferred to their offspring. Eventually, they were known as the American Horse, and when combined with Morgan, Standardbred, and Thoroughbred blood, produced the American Saddlebred as it is known today.

While the traditional gaits of walk, trot, and canter are innate, the Saddlebred is a breed apart, having inherited the ability to add additional gaits to its repertoire. These include the slow gait or running walk, the stepping pace, and the slow rack, which is when both hooves on either side are in turn lifted almost simultaneously. This means that, at certain moments, all four hooves are off the ground, which is spectacular when combined with the horse's high-stepping action.

This high-stepping carriage is sometimes falsely encouraged by keeping the feet long and building the feet up, while in other cases, the muscles under the dock are

OPPOSITE: Scripps Miramar Saddlebreds are presented in the famous New Year's Day Rose Parade in Pasadena, California, U.S.A.

ABOVE: The saddlebred is traditionally ridden in a Western-style bridle.

nicked to produce an unnaturally stiff and high tail-carriage: these are illegal practices in most countries of the world. The use of the tail brace also persists. This is sometimes fitted to a stabled horse in order that a high tail-carriage can be preserved; this, however, is at the expense of the horse's comfort when it is at rest. This practice should be modified or preferably banished if true recognition is to be achieved within the broader equestrian world.

The Saddlebred has a commanding presence and subtle expression of movement. The head is small and narrow, carried high, and the alert and intelligent expression is accentuated by the horse's fine pricked ears. The eyes are gentle but intelligent and the nose is straight with slightly flared nostrils. The neck is long and elegant and also carried high. The withers are high and run neatly into the back, which is fairly long, as is the barrel-shaped

body. The shoulders are narrower at the top than the bottom and slope to create the trademark fluid action. The tail-carriage is naturally high, joined to flat quarters flowing into strong and powerful loins.

The Saddlebred is biddable and easy to train. It is gentle and affectionate, loves people, and enjoys being handled. At the same time, it is spirited and proud, with a keen intelligence and an alert demeanor. It tends to become excitable under saddle.

Saddlebreds come in all the usual solid colors, including palomino and roan, and there is often a good deal of white on the head and legs. The coat, mane and tail are fine and silky in texture. The horses typically range in size from 15–16.1hh.

Saddlebreds are highly prized within the show ring, particularly in the harness and ridden classes in which they excel; but they are also capable of competing in other events, performing equally well as dressage horses and showjumpers.

LEFT: The American Saddlebred has a charming, biddable temperament and shows great affection towards its owners.

AMERICAN SHETLAND

As the name suggests, the American Shetland's ancestors were the native ponies of the Shetland Islands, situated off the northern coast of Scotland. In 1885, 75 ponies were imported to America by Eli Elliot, and were raised in the south-eastern states, where they thrived in spite of the warm, humid conditions. Their success led to the formation of the American Shetland Pony Club in 1888.

ABOVE, OPPOSITE & OVERLEAF: A well-trained American Shetland not only excels at driving, but its classic maximum height of only 46 inches (117cm) also makes it an excellent starter pony for a young child.

Today, the American Shetland is very different from its Scottish ancestor, being lighter in stature with longer, finer legs. This was achieved by crossing original Shetlands with small Arab, Thoroughbred, and Hackney breeds, resulting in a small horse rather than a stock pony.

The American Shetland now excels in various driven classes, such as the two-wheeled roadster, four-wheeled buggy, and light sulky. It is also good with children and will happily compete in pony as well as breed classes and hunter-pony events. It is ridden in either English or Western tack.

It possesses all the showy attributes of its small horse ancestors, combined with the strength and workmanlike character of the Scottish original. The head is longish, nearer to that of a horse than a pony; the nose is straight, the ears fairly long, and the eyes are also more like those of a horse. It has retained many of the original Shetland's characteristics, in that mane and high-set tail are furnished with thick, strong hair. The neck is quite short but the legs could be considered overlong, though they have retained their strength. The hooves retain the original Shetland strength and shape.

Having many of the attributes of the horse now in its make-up, the American Shetland has an equable temperament, and its small size makes it ideal for children to ride. It is reasonably hardy, making it easy to maintain.

American Shetlands come in all the usual solid colors, including roan, dun, and cream. They sometimes achieve heights in the region of 11.2hh.

APPALOOSA

The gene that produces the many permutations of spots in horses is an ancient one, as indicated in Cro-Magnon depictions of such horses in cave paintings. For many centuries, spotted horses were highly prized in Europe and Asia and they were often featured in Chinese art. The Spanish conquistadors brought their own such horses with them on their travels, introducing the spotted gene to the Americas when they arrived. After a time, some of these horses passed to Native Americans, in particular the Nez Percé, who lived in north-eastern Oregon along the Palouse river. The Nez Percé, probably the first to introduce selective

OPPOSITE, ABOVE & OVERLEAF: The Appaloosa is regarded as the archetypal American horse. Developed from European and American bloodlines, it has gained popularity as a versatile riding horse. Color patterns vary greatly.

breeding, followed strict guidelines to produce the best results. They called this meeting of European and native stock the Appaloosa – possibly America's oldest breed.

Settlers eventually eliminated the Nez Percé, and the Appaloosa was dispersed throughout the land, the strain becoming weakened through random breeding. Nowadays the Appaloosa is enjoying renewed popularity. It does not have to be spotted, however, although it is mandatory that

OPPOSITE: This foal's markings will develop more as it matures.

ABOVE: This mare displays the classic Appaloosa spots.

OVERLEAF: A beautifully-marked Appaloosa running free.

other criteria be present: the Appaloosa must have sclera around the eyeballs, striped hooves, and mottled skin beneath the hair.

The Appaloosa is a most versatile horse and looks good wearing Western tack. It is commonly used in Western events, such as roping, working cowhorse, and barrel-racing competitions. It is also used for showing, particularly

in Britain, in riding horse and colored horse classes, and is proficient at cross-country and jumping.

There are some obvious differences between American and European Appaloosas. The U.S. types have been crossed with Quarter Horses, with the result that their size and conformation are similar. In Europe, Appaloosas are rather larger, nearer to the size of a warmblood, making them ideal for jumping and dressage purposes. The type is also becoming popular in the United States.

After the formation of the Appaloosa Horse Club in 1938, a more modern type developed with the addition of Arabian bloodlines, while the Quarter Horse element produced Appaloosas that performed better in sprint racing and in halter competition. In fact, many cutting and reining horses resulted from old-type Appaloosas crossed on Arabian bloodlines.

OPPOSITE & ABOVE: Appaloosas vary in stature. These two are European versions which are similar in frame to the European warmblood.

RIGHT: American Appaloosas have more Arabian blood. This makes them finer and faster.

An infusion of Thoroughbred blood was added during the 1970s to produce horses more suited for racing. Many current breeders also attempt to breed away from the sparse, "rat tail" trait, with the result that modern Appaloosas have fuller manes and tails.

The Appaloosa is a workmanlike horse, with a fairly plain head and short, tapered ears. The eyes are alert and inquisitive, with the mandatory white rings or sclera around the eyeball rims. The neck and body are compact and well-muscled and the quarters are powerful with well-developed limbs. The tail and mane hair is relatively sparse. Hooves should be striped.

Appaloosas are great all-rounders: they are good-natured and hardy with plenty of stamina, speed and agility.

Color patterns include Blanket, which is a solid white area, normally over the quarters and loins, with a contrasting base color; Spots, when white or dark spots cover all or a portion of the body; Blanket with Spots, when there is a white blanket with dark spots within the white area, usually in the same color as the base color; Roan, when a lighter-colored area develops on the face and over the back, loins and quarters; Roan Blanket with Spots, when there is a roan blanket which has white and/or dark spots within the roan area; Solid, when a base color has no contrasting color in the form of an Appaloosa coat pattern. Appaloosas usually attain a height of between 14.2 and 15.2hh.

RIGHT: This finely bred foal will turn much darker as it becomes older. It is already showing a Blanket with Spots marking.

BANKER HORSE

The Banker is a breed of feral, domestic horse (*Equus ferus caballus*) found living on the Outer Bank Islands in North Carolina. Despite being feral, they are gentle, docile, and relatively easy to train. It is believed that Banker horses descended from Spanish horses brought to the Americas in the 16th century. It is thought they may have become feral after surviving shipwrecks or being abandoned on the islands by one of the exploratory expeditions led by Lucas Vázquez de Ayllón or Sir Richard Grenville. Populations are found on Ocracoke Island, Shackleford Banks, Currituck Banks, and in the Rachel Carson Estuarine Sanctuary.

The historical significance of the Banker is considered so important that they are are allowed to remain on the islands. They are managed by the National Park Service as well as other private organizations. It is important that they are not allowed to inbreed or over-populate the islands. They survive by grazing on marsh grasses, which supply them with water as well as food, supplemented by temporary freshwater pools.

The Banker has a broad face that tends to be straight or slightly convex. The chest is deep and narrow and the back is short with a sloped croup and low-set tail. Legs have an oval-shaped cannon bone, a trait considered indicative of "strong bone" or soundness. The callousities known as chestnuts are small, on some so tiny that they are barely detectable. Most Bankers have no chestnuts on the hind legs. The coat can be any color but is most often brown, bay, dun, or chestnut. Bankers have long-strided gaits and once trained make suitable pleasure horses for driving and trail riding. In the past they have been used for beach patrols and during World War II they were also used by coast guards. Owing to their gentle nature, they also make good children's ponies.

The typical Banker is relatively small, standing between 13.0 and 14.3hh.

BELOW: Bankers grazing among the sand dunes of North Carolina's Outer Bank Islands.

CHINCOTEAGUE

A feral resident of Assateague Island, the Chincoteague pony is a breed that lives wild. Assateague is owned by the federal government and is split by a fence at the Maryland-Virginia state line. A herd of around 150 ponies live on each side of the fence. The Maryland herd is managed by the National Park Service. The Virginia herd is managed by the Chincoteague Volunteer Fire Company. The horses survive by eating rough grasses and drinking from ponds.

According to legend, the Chincoteague descends from survivors of wrecked Spanish galleons off the Virginia

ABOVE & RIGHT: Chincoteauge ponies live in a feral state on Assateague Island on America's east coast.

coast. It is more likely though, they descend from stock released on the island by 17th-century colonists looking to escape livestock laws and taxes on the mainland.

The Chincoteague varies in its physical characteristics over the years as outside bloodlines have been added which have destorted some of the more traditional characteristics. In general though, the breed tends to have a straight or concave facial profile and a broad forehead. The shoulders are well-angled and the ribs well-spung. The chest is broard and the back is short. The croup is rounded and the tail is set on low. When trained Chincoteagues are intelligent and willing to please. Their health is good and they are easy to look after. They grow to on average to around 13.2–14.2hh.

ABOVE & RIGHT: Chincoteauge ponies are an attractive breed and make excellent riding ponies if domesticated.

CRIOLLO

The Spanish conquistadors brought the horse to the Americas and they could have done nothing better than to introduce the Arab, Barb and excellent Iberian. It is these three bloodlines that went into the making of the Criollo, the native horse of Argentina. For many hundreds of years the Criollo roamed the treeless plains (pampas) of Argentina, where pitiless natural selection helped to form it into one of the toughest horses in the world.

Criollos eventually came to be ridden by gauchos, or South American cowboys, who also used them as packhorses, having been quick to recognize their excellent hardiness, stamina, speed and resilience.

The Criollo is tough, can survive on next to nothing, and is an obedient worker. It is able to withstand some of the harshest conditions in the world.

Today, herds live in a semi-wild condition on the enormous ranches of South America, where they are caught and broken in as required. They are still used as stock and riding horses, and they make excellent polo ponies when crossed with Thoroughbreds.

Rigorous endurance tests to evaluate Criollos for breeding are used where horses ride over a 466-mile (750-km) course, carrying a load of 245lb (111kg), to be completed in a set time. During this time, the horses feed only on what they can forage for themselves,

OPPOSITE, ABOVE & OVERLEAF: The Criollo is relatively rare, although fortunately the demand for Criollos is growing, notably in the United States.

and they are checked by veterinarians once the test has been completed.

The Criollo's toughness is more than obvious from its stocky exterior. The head is broad with wide-set eyes and the nose is slightly dished. It has fairly large ears. The neck is well-developed with a wide back and chest and strong quarters. The back is also short, with sloping shoulders, and the short, sturdy legs possess plenty of bone.

Color is most commonly dun, with a black mane and tail, an eel stripe down the center of the back, and zebra markings on the legs. Other colors are chestnut, bay, black, roan, gray, piebald, skewbald, and palomino. Height is from 14–15hh.

FALABELLA

It is said that the Falabella's ancestors were first seen in the 19th century, interspersed with the herds of South American Indians. But it was more probably the creation of the Falabella family, at their ranch near Buenos Aires in Argentina, over a century ago. The breed was established by first crossing small Arab and Thoroughbred stallions with Shetland Pony mares. Then, using selective breeding, it was made ever smaller.

The Falabella is not a pony: it is a miniature horse with all the conformation and character of a horse. Because of excessive in-breeding, however, the conformation of some individuals is far from ideal; consequently they tend to look

BELOW, OPPOSITE & OVERLEAF: The tiny Falabella is not classified as a pony but as a small horse, although one that is capable of being ridden only by very small children.

rather odd. They are also weak for their size and can be ridden only by the smallest children. Today, breeders are attempting to rectify these faults and are generally trying to improve the breed.

Being affectionate, Falabellas make ideal pets and are sometimes allowed even into peoples' homes because of their small size. They are popular in special in-hand showing classes and are capable of pulling small carts.

Correctly bred, a Fallabella should resemble a miniature Thoroughbred or Arab, though its Shetland ancestry may occasionally come to the fore. The head is refined and horse-

OPPOSITE, BELOW & OVERLEAF: Falabellas come in a variety of colors.

like, with a straight nose, and small, flared nostrils. The small ears are set wide apart, and the eyes are kind. The body is medium-length, with a slim frame, and the legs are fine, similar to those of a Thoroughbred.

The Falabella is a delightful breed. It provides all the pleasures of a larger breed but at a lower cost; this is particularly true as far as land requirements are concerned. Its constitution, however, is less that robust and it requires the same care that one would give to any finely bred horse. It is amenable, docile and obedient.

Falabellas come in all solid colors, as well as gray and roan, and Appaloosa markings are also common. Ideally, they should stand no taller than 30in (76cm) from the ground.

KENTUCKY MOUNTAIN SADDLE HORSE

The Kentucky Mountain Saddle Horse originates in the U.S. state of Kentucky. It is related to the Tennessee Walking Horse and other gaited breeds. It was developed as an all-rounder and farm horse.

The Kentucky Moutain is a mid-sized horse, with a well-muscled and compact build. The breed has a flat facial profile, a mid-length, well-arched neck, a deep chest and well-sloped shoulders. They are known to be easy keepers and tough. To be registered, Kentucky Mountain Saddle Horses must demonstrate a gentle temperament and willing disposition.

The breed is known for a natural ambling gait, called the single-foot, which replaces the trot seen in a majority of horse breeds. Both gaits are an intermediate speed between a walk and a canter or gallop; ambling gaits are four-beat gaits, whereas the trot is a two-beat gait. The extra footfalls provide additional smoothness to a rider because the horse always has at least one foot on the ground. This minimizes movement of the horse's topline and removes the bounce of a two-beat gait, caused by a moment of suspension followed by the jolt of two feet hitting the ground as the horse shifts from one pair of legs to the other. The value of an intermediate speed is that the horse conserves energy. More than thirty horse breeds are "gaited," able to perform a four-beat ambling gait, and some can also trot.

The breed comes in a variety of solid colors with many eye-catching palomino, and chocolate colored coats. Chocolates are a deep brown with a pale flaxen mane and tail. The registry allows white markings on the face such as stars and blazes and stockings and socks below the knee. They have generous flowing manes and tails.

Early Kentucky Mountain Saddle Horses were small, so two size classifications were created: pony size, 11–13.3hh; and horse size, 14hh and up.

RIGHT: A chocolate-colored Kentucky Mountain Saddle Horse.

MANGALARGA MARCHADOR

Brazil and Portugal have been closely connected for centuries, and at one time they even had the same ruler, Don João VI, in around 1815. It was he who was responsible for bringing quality Portuguese and Spanish horses to Brazil, particularly the Andalusian and the Altér Real.

The Brazilian Mangalarga is a direct descendant of one particular Altér Real stallion, which was mated with Criollo mares, though more Altér Real, Barb, and Andalusian were eventually added to improve the breed. The result is neat, lightly built, and strongly reminiscent of the Barb but with the rolling gait of the Spanish breeds.

The Mangalarga is most often used on the enormous estancias of Brazil, where its fifth gait, known as the *marcha*, makes it fast but comfortable to ride. It has a smooth, stable walk, canter, and gallop, as well as a natural diagonal (*batida*) or lateral (*picada*) four-beat gait.

The Mangalarga's head is high and proud, with medium-length ears, intelligent eyes, and a nose that is straight with flaring nostrils. The back is long with strong loins and neat quarters; the shoulders are sloping with a deep girth, and there are well-muscled legs with hard hooves.

The Mangalarga has incredible stamina, and this enables it to work all day and cover huge distances. It is good-natured, willing and obedient. Coat colors are usually bay, gray, chestnut, and roan. Height is around 15hh.

BELOW, OPPOSITE & OVERLEAF: Today, the Mangalarga Marchador is used for endurance, trail riding, jumping, and polo. It is an excellent and versatile riding and showing horse.

MISSOURI FOX TROTTER

The Missouri Fox Trotter was developed in the 19th century by settlers in Missouri and Arkansas. Initially, its purpose was to be a general riding horse, with the speed and endurance to cope with difficult terrain. The foundation stock for the breed was the Morgan, which was infused with Thoroughbred and Arab as well as Iberian blood.

As horses with elaborate gaits became more popular, the breed was later mated with the Saddlebred and Tennessee Walking Horse, which greatly improved its elegance, bearing and paces, including its foxtrot gait; this is basically a diagonal gait, like the trot, in which the horse appears to be walking with the front legs while trotting with the hind.

In the early days, the Fox Trotter had been a useful competitor in racing, but increasingly has reverted to its use as a general riding horse.

A stud book for the breed was eventually opened in 1948. The breed society, however, put in place strict guidelines that the Missouri Fox Trotter should have no artificial aids to influence and enhance its gait, such as nicking or setting the tail; consequently its action is not as pronounced or extravagant as that of the American Saddlebred, for example. The breed is popular in the United States, where it is used for general riding, showing and endurance.

The head is a little plain, with a straight nose and a square muzzle with large open nostrils. The ears are medium-length and alert, and the eyes have a kind but

BELOW, OPPOSITE & OVERLEAF: The Missouri Fox Trotter was developed by settlers in the early 19th century. It quickly developed into a gaited breed appreciated for its stock horse abilities, stamina, and smooth gaits.

intelligent expression. The neck is medium-length and fairly well-developed, with prominent withers; the back is short, with strong loins and hindquarters. The tail is set fairly low, and the legs are long with large joints and well-shaped, strong hooves.

The Missouri Fox Trotter has a charming, easy-going manner. It is willing and obedient with excellent stamina and endurance. It comes in colors and can also be part-colored. Height is from 14–16hh.

MORGAN

One of America's most famous and versatile breeds, all Morgans can be traced back to just one stallion called Figure. Figure was later renamed Justin Morgan after its owner, Thomas Justin Morgan, a tavern keeper and singing teacher, who supplemented his income by breeding stallions.

The colt was born in around 1790 in Vermont. It is thought that its sire was probably a Welsh Cob, called True Briton, though little is known of the dam, other than that she may have had Oriental and Thoroughbred blood.

Thomas Justin Morgan was so impressed with his stallion's looks and personality that he eventually decided to put him to stud. The results were remarkable in that a foal the image of its father was always produced no matter

BELOW: This proud buckskin Morgan foal is eye-catching to say the least.

OPPOSITE: The Morgan is one of the first horse breeds ever to have been developed in the United States. It is an attractive animal, and often has a long, flowing mane and tail.

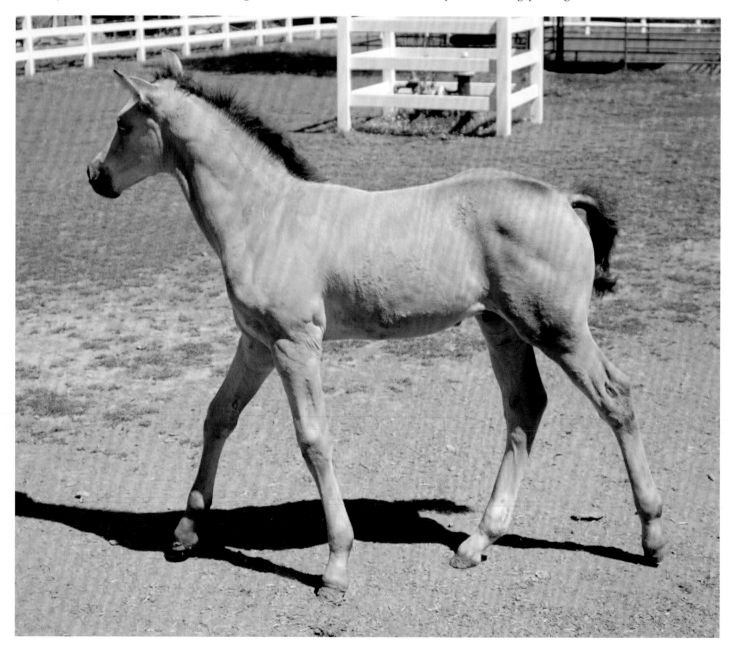

what mare Justin Morgan covered. The sire's prowess as a marvelous harness and riding horse, moreover, seemed to be replicated in the offspring, the performance of each of them being second to none. In fact, all were amazed that such a significant and impressive breed could have developed from a single stallion.

Morgans are just as versatile today – used in harness competitions, shows, driving and trail-riding. They are strong and hard-working, and have a spirited but tractable nature.

The head should provide immediate evidence of quality, with beautiful and expressive eyes. The muzzle is small and the profile straight or slightly dished. The neck is well-crested and the shoulders strong. The hindquarters are large and strong and the legs sturdy.

LEFT, ABOVE & OPPOSITE: Morgans are strong, courageous, and hardworking. They have a spirited but tractable nature.

A type known as the Park Morgan is bred particularly for its high-stepping action. Another type is the Pleasure Morgan, whose action is less exaggerated. All solid colors are acceptable in this breed. They stand somewhere between 14 and 15.2hh.

MUSTANG

Although horses had once been present in North America, by the time the conquistadors arrived in the Americas in the 16th century, the indigenous prehistoric horses had long been extinct. The Spanish brought Iberian horses with them in their ships, derived mainly from Arabs and Barbs. Many of these sleek, desert-bred and resilient horses were allowed to wander off, spreading into North America and forming feral rather than wild herds. They became known as Mustangs.

BELOW, OPPOSITE & OVERLEAF: The Mustang is the free-roaming horse of the Amercian West. It descends from horses brought to the Americas by the Spanish. As it was once domesticated, it is classified as feral rather than wild.

PINTO/PAINT HORSE

The Pinto or Paint Horse (from the Spanish *pintado*, meaning "painted"), like many of the old American breeds, is descended from Iberian horses that were brought to the Americas by the conquistadors in the 16th century. They are sometimes referred to as "calico" horses in America.

In England and other Anglophone countries they are referred to as "piebalds" (black-and-white) or "skewbalds" (any other color and white) because their coats, of any solid color, are heavily mottled with white; alternatively they are merely referred to as colored horses, though in the United States the Pinto is regarded as a separate breed.

BELOW, OPPOSITE & OVERLEAF: The Pinto or Paint Horse is used in a variety of equestrian disciplines, including Western pleasure, reining, and other Western events. It is also known to be a good showjumper.

ABOVE, OPPOSITE & OVERLEAF: The Pinto's coat is always white with colored patterning, making it one of the most striking of all the breeds.

The original Spanish horses were allowed to revert to a feral condition and gradually extended into North America, where they roamed uninhabited lands and Western deserts. Once domesticated by Native Americans, however, they became greatly revered; in fact, it was believed that the Pinto even possessed magic powers.

Ranchers also adopted these hardy horses, whose stamina and agility made them excellent for work over great distances. Today, they are still used as workhorses but also at rodeos; they are also used for trail-riding and showing and as all-round riding horses.

The Pinto has a fine head and graceful, well-defined neck. The ears are alert and of medium length, while the eyes indicate spirit and intelligence. They are usually quite short in the back, with long, strong legs and hard, tough hooves. They are hardy and agile.

The Pinto is well-known for its striking coat, which can be black, chestnut, brown, bay, dun, sorrel, palomino, gray, or roan, patched with large areas of white. There are three distinctive types of coat pattern: Tobiano, in which the head is like that of any solid-colored horse, but there are round or oval spots resembling shields running over the neck and chest. One or both flanks may be colored white or a color can predominate, while the tail is often bi-colored; Overo, which is predominantly dark or white, though the white shouldn't cross the back between withers and tail. The head should be white with scattered irregular markings on the rest of the body. At least one leg should be dark and the tail is usually one color; Tovero is a mixture of the two. Pintos stand between 14.2 and 15.2hh.

PASO FINO

Coming from Puerto Rico, the foundation of the Paso Fino is old Spanish or Iberian stock. It has the same bloodlines, inherited from horses brought to the Americas by the Spanish conquistadors in the 16th century; in terms of character and conformation, however, different environments have caused slight variations in their evolution.

The Paso Fino is a naturally gaited horse, like the Peruvian Paso or Stepping Horse and another lesser-known Colombian breed, and although it is predominantly a working horse, these attributes make it stand out from the crowd. Aficionados claim that because of its natural, even, four-beat gait, that can be performed at varying speeds, it is the smoothest riding horse in the world. The classic *fino* is a collected gait, executed with a rapid footfall that covers little ground. The *paso corto* is a moderate gait, useful in trail riding, and the *paso largo* is a fast gait in which the horse can reach speeds equivalent to a canter or slow gallop. Not all

OPPOSITE, ABOVE & OVERLEAF: The Paso Fino is prized for its smooth, natural, four-beat, lateral gait. It is renowned for its endurance and comfortable ride.

Paso Finos can perform the classic *fino*, but the majority perform the other gaits with ease.

There are another two variants: the *sobre paso*, a more natural gait in which the horse is allowed a loose rein and is relaxed, and which is used in general riding rather than the

PERUVIAN PASO

As its name suggests, the Peruvian Paso, or Peruvian Stepping Horse, comes from Peru. It shares much of its descent with the Paso Fino, the national horse of Puerto Rico, the foundation of both breeds being Barb and old Spanish or Iberian stock brought to the Americas by the conquistadors in the 16th century.

The Peruvian Paso has adapted well to its environment and is able to carry riders great distances over dangerous mountain terrain with safety and comfort. It has also

adapted to the high altitudes of the Andes Range and has a larger, stronger heart and greater lung capacity than other breeds; this enables it to function energetically at heights where oxygen is scarce.

Like the other Paso breeds, the Peruvian has the natural ability to perform the attractive four-beat lateral gaits that make riding long distances so comfortable for the rider without tiring the horse. There are three gaits: the *paso corto*, used for practical purposes; the *paso fino*, an exaggerated slow gait used in the show ring and in parades, which has the appearance almost of slow motion; and the *paso largo*, which is fast. These traits are passed from mare to foal and are completely natural, needing no artificial aids. Once a person becomes accustomed to the gaits (the horse never trots or gallops) the Peruvian makes an excellent riding horse.

In stature, the Peruvian is similar to its cousin the Paso Fino. The head is fine and resembles that of the Barb, with shapely pricked ears and a proud, alert look. The nostrils are readily dilated, presumably to allow as much oxygen as possible to be taken in. The body has all the evidence of a Spanish inheritance and is similar to the Andalusian's. The legs are sturdy, quite long, and well-muscled with hard hooves.

While the Peruvian Paso is hardy and energetic, it is also even-tempered and intelligent. It is an obedient and willing worker. Peruvians may be any color, but bay or chestnut, with white on the head and legs, is permitted. The mane and tail are abundant, with fine, lustrous hair that may be straight or curly. They range in height between 14 and 15.2hh.

LEFT: The Peruvian Paso shares much of its ancestry with the Paso Fino. Its is known for its smooth ride.

OPPOSITE & OVERLEAF: Peruvian Pasos being ridden in traditional tack. It is notable that a crupper is always used in conjuction with a Peruvian saddle.

ABOVE & OPPOSITE: Ideally, the Pony of the Americas should display style and substance, beauty and symmetry, being well-balanced and correct in all aspects of its conformation.

easy to handle. It is also strong enough to carry a small adult and is used in endurance, trail-riding and showjumping, as well as trotting and pony flat-racing.

The head is very Arab, with a broad forehead, small pricked ears, and a straight or slightly dished nose. The eyes are large and kind. The body is of medium length, with a good sloping shoulder, well-developed quarters, and fine but strong legs. It is strong and hardy, with a calm but willing disposition. It shares similar markings with the Appaloosa, and stands between 11.2 and 14hh.

QUARTER HORSE

It is no surprise that the Quarter Horse holds a place of pride in the hearts of all American horse lovers, seeing that it was the first breed to become established in the United States.

The Quarter Horse's origins can be traced back 500 years to the time when the Spanish conquistadors brought Iberian and Oriental horses to Florida. English colonists

LEFT, ABOVE, OPPOSITE & OVERLEAF: The Quarter Horse comes in two main body types: the stock type and the hunter or racing type. The stock type, although agile, is shorter, more compact, stocky and well-muscled, while the hunter or racing type, bearing more of a resemblance to the Thoroughbred, is somewhat taller and smoother muscled than the stock type.

eventually acquired these horses from Chickasaw Indians, which they crossed with their own English horses, mainly Thoroughbreds, then refined them again with more Thoroughbred blood.

of steel and amazing agility. They also had plenty of cow sense, having worked the bullrings of Portugal and Spain for generations. Today, racing predominates, but their use in rodeos, trailing and as all-round family mounts is widespread across the United States, Canada, Australia, and even parts of Europe.

Quarter Horses can be quite large animals, due to the influence of the Thoroughbred in their breeding. The head is relatively small and the eyes are bright and set far apart. The neck, hindquarters and back are extremely muscular, which makes the feet appear relatively small.

Quarter Horses are easy to maintain, and are enthusiastic, honest and energetic. Their coats may be of any color, and their height range is between 14.2 and 16hh.

LEFT & ABOVE: The Quarter Horse excels at sprinting short distances.

STANDARDBRED

The Standardbred is famous for its trotting and pacing abilities and is widely used in harness racing throughout the world. The breed dates back 200 years, when trotting races had become sufficiently popular to warrant a breeding program of their own.

The founding sire of today's Standardbred was Messenger, a gray Thoroughbred, born in 1780 and imported to Philadelphia in 1788. While Messenger was bred for traditional racing at a gallop, his own sire,

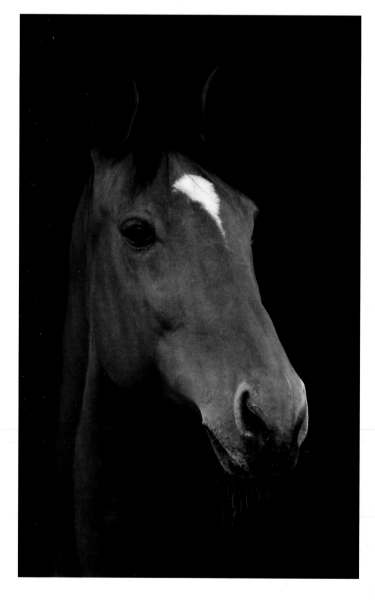

ABOVE, RIGHT & OVERLEAF: The Standardbred possesses considerable stamina and endurance. It is similar in stature to the Thoroughbred, but is usually smaller with a longer and lower body.

Mambrino, had been responsible for a long dynasty of famous trotting coachhorses in England.

Messenger worked at stud for about 20 years and became famous for producing strong, talented trotters. Meanwhile, during the mid-1800s in New England, the Morgan breed was being used to produce a line of smaller trotters with a straight up-and-down action. The high-stepping action of the Morgan line was then combined with the long-reaching stride of the Messenger, which increased the performance of the Standardbred no end.

The trot of a Standardbred appears huge in comparison with that of ordinary breeds and is a gait whereby the legs are moved in diagonal pairs. The "pace," however, is peculiar to this breed and is a gait where the horse moves its legs in lateral pairs. While the trot comes naturally to all horses, the pace generally has to be taught, although some Standardbreds seem able to pace from birth. Pacing is quicker than trotting as it allows the stride to be longer and more economical.

The term Standardbred was introduced in 1879 and derives from the time standard that was set to test the ability of harness racers. Originally, the Standardbred horse was required to cover a mile in 2 minutes and 30 seconds. Since this first standard was set, improved

OPPOSITE, ABOVE & OVERLEAF: The Standardbred tends to be more placid than the Thoroughbred. It is known for its honesty, steady, tractable nature, and its love for human companionship.

breeding has enabled the modern Standardbred to beat this target easily.

The head is in proportion to the horse's body and the eyes are kind, while the ears are indicative of its alertness. The horse is muscular overall, with a well-sprung barrel, sloping shoulder, and a strong back. The legs resemble those of the Thoroughbred, though they are rather more solid, with larger joints; the hooves are large and strong.

The Standardbred has an excellent temperament and is quite a placid horse when away from the race track. When racing, however, it is highly competitive, and displays great stamina and unbounding energy. They come in all solid colors, but mainly bay, black, brown, and chestnut. Size ranges from 14.2–17.2hh.

TENNESSEE WALKING HORSE

The Tennessee (or Plantation) Walking Horse originated in the deep south of the United States and was recognized as the ideal utility breed to carry plantation owners around their large estates. The smooth, gliding gait of the "Walker" (as the breed is also known) provided hours of comfort in

ABOVE, OPPOSITE & OVERLEAF: The Tennessee Walking Horse is famous for its comfortable and unusual gaits. It is extensively used for pleasure riding and in the show ring.

156

the saddle; the movement is performed from the elbow rather than the shoulder, thus transmitting the minimum of movement to the rider. Although still widely ridden for pleasure, the Walker is nowadays extensively bred for the show ring, and it is also used as a general riding and harness horse.

In fact there are two or three characteristic gaits, the flat-footed walk, the running walk, and the canter. The first horse perceived to have this natural talent was foaled in 1837, but it took another 50 years or so to establish the breed as it is today.

The Thoroughbred, Standardbred, American Saddlebred, Narragansett Pacer and Morgan bloodlines all

played their part in establishing this distinctive breed, but it was one stallion, born in 1886, that became its foundation stallion. It possessed all the desired qualities, such as the delightful temperament and the characteristic gaits. Most of the offspring inherited their sire's traits and he subsequently enjoyed many successful years at stud. Once a breed association had become established, approximately 300,000 horses were registered.

The Walker has a large head with a straight profile, gentle eyes, and pointed ears. The neck is arched and muscular, with a broad base that enables the head to be carried elegantly high. The breed has plenty of bone, which adds to its sturdiness, and a short-coupled and level topline. The limb joints are well-made, with particularly powerful hocks that allow the hindlegs to step well under the body.

ABOVE, OPPOSITE & OVERLEAF: The Tennessee Walker is frequently to be seen in programs featuring handicapped riders, and people with back problems often find it a more comfortable horse to ride.

The tail, which is usually left long, is often nicked and set artificially high.

Walkers are naturally gentle and calm, but it is their unusual gaits for which they are most famous. Although the gaits are inherited, they need to be developed by further training. The flat walk, running walk and canter are natural to the breed. The running walk has several variations: the rack, the stepping pace, the fox-trot and single-foot.

Tennessee Walking Horses may be any color, but especially black, chestnut, brown, gray, roan or bay. Height is between 15 and 17h.

CHAPTER SIX
HORSES OF EUROPE

"Horses - if God made anything more beautiful, he kept it for himself."

—Anonymous

ALTÉR REAL

Portugal has two breeds of horses, both of which are used in the bullring and in *haute école* classical riding: the famous Lusitano and the lesser known, but no less noble, Altér Real. The breed had its beginnings in the 18th century, when 300 Andalusian mares, intended for the specific requirements of the Portuguese court in Lisbon, were brought from Jerez in Spain to the royal house of Braganza's

stud at Vila de Portel in Portugal. After eight years, the stud moved to Altér do Chão, which gave the horse the first part of its name, the second part meaning royal. For many years the breed excelled not only in classical disciplines but also as a quality carriage horse.

The Altér Real breed came under jeopardy during the Napoleonic invasion of 1809–10, when troops stole the best horses from the stud, drastically reducing their numbers. Then, in 1832, King Miguel abdicated and much of the stud's land became subject to confiscation.

In later years, measures were taken to improve the existing stock by breeding it with Thoroughbreds, Normans, and Arabs; this, however, only served to weaken the breed, causing much loss of its original character. In the late 19th century, however, the Spanish Zapata family introduced more Andalusian and Carthusian blood, and this reversed much of the earlier damage.

The breed finally obtained the protection it deserved in the early 20th century, when steps were taken to restore it to its former glory. This was achieved with the help of Dr. Ruy d'Andrade who, with two stallions and a handful of mares, founded a top-quality Altér Real stud. He eventually handed the stud over to the Portuguese Ministry of Agriculture, which administers the breeding program today. The Altér Real is still used in haute école and general riding.

The head has all the distinctive Iberian qualities of the Lusitano and Andalusian, having a fine head with a slightly dished nose, medium-length shapely ears, and a lively, intelligent eye. The neck is short but well-positioned, with a pronounced, arched crest. The shoulders are sloping and the chest is well-developed. The back is short and strong with ample quarters. The legs are hard and very tough, the upper parts being well-muscled with large joints ending in small but well-shaped hooves.

OPPOSITE & RIGHT: The Altér Real is still much in demand as a classical riding horse and many are bred in studs all over Portugal.

The Altér Real has a high-stepping action which is most attractive: this, coupled with its strength and power, makes it appear much larger than it actually is. Unlike its Iberian brothers, the Altér Real is not suitable for beginners in that it has inherited a fiery and lively temperament from non-Iberian blood added in the early 19th century. It is responsive and learns quickly but needs a competent and experienced rider in order to excel. Coat color is usually bay and height is between 15 and 16hh.

ANDALUSIAN

This celebrated Spanish breed is one of the oldest to have been handled and ridden by man: there is further evidence of this fact in cave paintings, which confirm that horses of this kind were present in the Iberian Peninsula in around 5000 BC.

The Andalusian's lineage stems from the Sorraia Pony, which still exists in Iberia, and the North African Barb, with additional Arab and Oriental strains. It evolved in Iberia, most of which was then known as Andalusia, at the time of the Moorish occupation of 711. The result was a horse with a head-carriage that was high and proud, and paces that were extravagant and highly placed.

The Andalusian was particularly valued as a warhorse, having all the qualities that enabled it to perform well in battle. (It is interesting to note that El Cid's mount, Babieca, was an Andalusian.) Later, in the 16th century, the conquistadors brought the horse with them to the Americas, where it became the basis of all American breeds, which also share lineage with the Lusitano, Carthusian and Altér Real.

BELOW & OPPOSITE: The Andalusian is one of the purest breeds of horses present in the world today. It shares similarities with the closely related Lusitano breed.

Today, the Andalusian can still be traced back to these lines, the purest and most beautiful of which are still referred to as *caballos Cartujanos*. Their extreme rarity forced the Spanish government to ban their export for over 100 years, but the embargo was lifted in the 1960s, and they now enjoy popularity around the world.

Today, the Andalusian is used for bullfighting and display riding, where its power and agility allow it to execute the intricate movements with ease. They excel at advanced classical dressage and at showjumping and are also useful for general riding and driving. They are often to be seen in hand in the show ring.

The Andalusian bloodline is evident in around 80 percent of modern breeds and has had a particular influence on the Connemara, native to Ireland, the Lipizzaner of the Balkans, and the Cleveland Bay and Welsh Cob of the British Isles. However, its popularity was not to last, and in around 1700 the Andalusian's heavy, robust conformation fell from favor, when lighter, sleeker animals, used for hunting and racing, became more fashionable. Andalusians suffered even more when a plague and famine almost wiped them out; a few survived in the Carthusian monasteries of Castello, Jerez and Seville, where breeding from the best of the animals continued.

OPPOSITE, ABOVE & RIGHT: The Andalusian excels in the difficult maneuvers of haute école, *for which it remains famous today.*

These muscular horses have great presence and beauty. The neck is heavy, with a well-developed crest. The mane is abundant and should be kept long. The head-carriage is noble and high, the forehead wide with expressive, medium-length ears. The eyes are dark-brown and gentle, the nostrils are flared, and the jaw is large and well-muscled. The withers are well-rounded and the shoulder is long and sloping. The chest is broad, the croup rounded, and the low-set tail is thick and long. The body is rounded and short-coupled, adding to the overall strength. The legs are strong with large joints and the hooves are rounded and compact.

The Andalusian is famous for its extravagant paces. Movement is elevated and extended, making the horse look as if it were floating on air. All paces are smooth, showy and spectacular.

Andalusians are proud and courageous, and although spirited to ride, they have amiable temperaments. They have soft mouths, making them extremely obedient when ridden correctly.

Gray and bay coats are most in evidence, but others are accepted by the Andalusian Horse Association. In Spain, according to the studbook, only gray, bay, and black are acceptable. Height is between 15 and 16.2hh.

BELOW, OPPOSITE & OVERLEAF: Throughout its history, the Andalusian has been known for its prowess and courage as a warhorse.

BUDENNY

The Budenny, or Budyonny, is a relatively young breed, created by the Russians to fit the basic criteria of a Perfect Russian Horse, a standard which is centuries old. A Russian horse should be an excellent all-rounder, equally at home ridden as pulling a carriage. Development of the breed began in 1921 when the devastation of the First World War and the Revolution made it clear that a good cavalry horse was required. The horse was named after Marshal Budenny (1883–1973), who was responsible for the breed's development.

As a cavalry horse it was obliged to satisfy a number of requirements: it needed enormous stamina, a good turn of speed, and the ability to jump; obedience and an equable nature were also needed, as well as great courage. The breeding program took place at Rostov where there was a military stud. The breed is based on Don and Chernomor mares crossed with Thoroughbred stallions; Chernomors

BELOW, OPPOSITE & OVERLEAF: The Budenny was originally bred as a cavalry horse. Today it is mainly used for competition and as a general riding horse.

are similar to Dons, though rather lighter. They also introduced Kazakh and Kirgiz blood, though this was not as successful. The breed was eventually recognized and was registered in 1949.

Today the Budenny is used as a performance horse and in all disciplines including racing, endurance, and showjumping. It is also used in harness.

The Budenny bears a close resemblance to the Thoroughbred, being tall and powerful with good bone and muscle. The head is medium-sized and sits well on the neck. The nose is straight or slightly concave and the nostrils are wide. The ears are of medium size and the eyes

are bold. The neck is long and set high and the withers are also high. The back is fairly short and is inclined to flatten towards the withers. The loins are wide, medium-length and muscular. The croup is usually long. The shoulder is of medium length and sloping. The legs are clean and strong and the hooves well-shaped and hard.

Due to its military breeding, the Budenny has plenty of courage and spirit. It is also obedient and has a good disposition.

Budennys are nearly always chestnut, with an iridescent sheen inherited from the Don. Bays and browns occasionally appear.

Height is approximately 16hh.

BELOW: The Budenny is strong and powerful. It excels in showjumping, eventing, and endurance competitions.

CAMARGUE

The salt marshes and lagoons of the Rhône delta, located south of Arles in France, are home to a race of semi-wild horses that spend their time grazing the sparse vegetation. This is a very ancient breed that bears a striking resemblance to the primitive horses painted on cave-walls at Lascaux in prehistoric times. The Camargue's qualities were appreciated by Roman invaders on their way to the Iberian Peninsula, with the result that connections were inevitably made with Spanish breeds.

BELOW & OPPOSITE: It would be unthinkable to visit the Camargue without seeing the famous white horses that have been roaming there for centuries.

The breed was further enhanced in the 19th century by infusions of Postier Breton, Arab, Thoroughbred, and Anglo-Arab bloodlines, though they seem to have had little bearing on the horses' overall appearance.

There is a round-up in the Camargue every year, when suitable horses are selected for riding purposes and

BELOW, OPPOSITE & OVERLEAF: The Camargue is an ancient breed. It is generally considered to be one of the oldest horse breeds in the world. They inhabit the salt marshes and lagoons of the Rhône delta in southern France.

substandard animals are culled: this may seem ruthless but there is no doubt that it has led to improvements in the breed.

Camargue horses are traditionally ridden by the *gardians* (Camargue cowboys), who use them for herding the famous black bulls of the region and for festivals in which their dazzling feats of horsemanship are displayed. The horses are also used for trekking the region, now a popular tourist attraction.

The head of the Camargue (Camaguais) is rather square, with a broad forehead, short, broad ears, and expressive eyes. The neck is short and well-developed, the shoulder upright, and the back is short with a low-set tail. The legs are strong and the hooves well-shaped and tough. The mane and tail are particularly abundant.

Camargues make obedient riding horses; they are extremely agile and have the ability to turn sharply at full gallop. As trekking ponies they are sure-footed and have plenty of stamina. They never quite lose their independent spirit, however, and something of their wild inheritance is always retained. They are invariably white (gray), though other colors sometimes appear. Foals are born dark but their coats grow lighter as they mature. Height is from 13.1–14.2hh.

BELOW: Camargue horses are ridden by cowboys known as gardians *who manage the black bull population of the area.*

OPPOSITE: Camargue horses are semi-feral, however once trained, they are are suitable for many equestrian disciplines.

CLYDESDALE

The establishment of the Scottish Clydesdale began in the late-17th century when Lanarkshire farmers and various dukes of Hamilton supposedly imported Flemish stallions, ancestors of the Brabant, to Scotland. The farmers were skillful breeders and mated them with native heavy draft mares already in existence; over the next 100 years or so, English Shire, Friesian, and Cleveland Bay blood was also added. The result was known as the Clydesdale and it was highly prized as a draft horse. The Clydesdale Horse Society was established in 1877, almost a century and a half after the breed first began to evolve.

BELOW, OPPOSITE & OVERLEAF: The outstanding characteristics of the famous Clydesdale are a combination of weight, strength, size, and activity.

The breed soon became popular as a general farm horse and also for hauling loads over long and short distances; Clydesdales could be found in most major cities of Scotland, the North of England and Northern Ireland, as well as in agricultural areas. In fact, the horse became popular the world over, when considerable numbers were imported to North America, Canada, and Australia.

Clydesdales are very different from the usual heavy draft horses, which tend to be plain-looking and squat; in fact, it looks positively refined, having a short-coupled body, long legs, and a high head-carriage. As with all heavy horses, the Clydesdale breed began to decline with the development of motorized transport and reached an even lower ebb in the 1960s and '70s. A few families kept the breed going, however, and today numbers are rising, although the Clydesdale continues to be classified as "at risk" by the Rare Breeds Society. Today they are highly valued in the show ring as well as in harness; as dray horses, they often take part in displays, and are even used to pull wedding carriages.

The head is proudly held, and the medium, well-shaped ears are pricked and alert; the eyes are kind and intelligent. It has a slightly Roman nose and the nostrils are large. The neck is long and well-set, with a high crest leading to high withers. The back is slightly concave and short and the quarters are well-developed and powerful. The legs are straight and long with plenty of feathering. The feet are large and require careful shoeing if contracted heels are not to develop.

These charming horses are energetic with an alert, cheerful air. They are even-tempered and enjoy company. They are extremely strong with a lively action and a slight tendency to dish.

Clydesdales can be bay, brown, and black and usually have white patches all the way up the legs and under the belly, which can turn roan in places. They are usually around 16.2hh, but some males may reach 17hh or more.

LEFT & OPPOSITE: A couple of hundred years ago the Clydesdale was a common sight, working on farms and hauling heavy loads over great distances.

OVERLEAF: Nowadays these impressive horses are more likely to be seen in the show ring or in ceremonies. These famous Budweiser Clydesdales are on show in the Grand Floral Parade during the Portland Rose Festival, Portland, Oregon.

CONNEMARA

The Connemara is Ireland's only native breed, although it is not indigenous to the country. It is thought that it was brought to Ireland 2,500 years ago when the Celts settled in Ireland and brought their ponies with them. The Celts were traders and traveled to and from Mediterranean ports, which makes it likely that their ponies were of Oriental

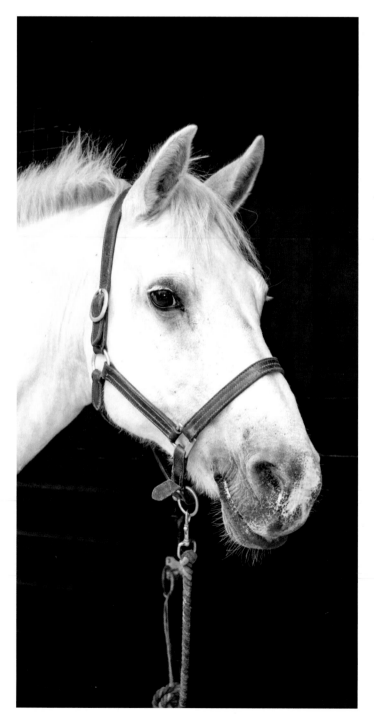

descent, probably Barb. In medieval times these horses were bred with the Irish Hobeye, which was a much coveted riding horse, famous for its speed, agility and endurance.

Legend has it that further blood was added to the breed when the Spanish Armada sank off the coast of Ireland and

LEFT, ABOVE & OVERLEAF: Connemaras are excellent all-round riding ponies. They are naturally good at jumping, to the extent that they are often bred with other horses to make showjumpers.

RIGHT: Connemaras still graze semi-wild on Ireland's wild Atlantic coast.

DON

The Don is Russia's most famous breed. It originated in the harsh Russian steppes, where it once roamed in herds, surviving the freezing winters and torrid summers with nothing but sparse vegetation for food.

The original steppes breed, known as the Old Don, was bred with various Orientals, such as the Arab, Karabakh and Turkmene, and Orlov and Thoroughbred were added to improve its conformation and provide it with incredible stamina.

The horse was the preferred mount of the Don Cossacks; it was also used by the Russian army, and its extreme toughness made it particularly popular with wolf-hunters. Today, the Don's hardy constitution makes it an excellent endurance horse. It is also used to improve other breeds.

The overall picture of the Don is one of strength and robustness. The head is fairly small and neat, the slightly dished or straight nose clearly indicating its Arab heritage. Ears are small and shapely and the eyes are large and intelligent. The neck is set high and should be arched; however, many have ewe necks. The back is fairly long, straight and wide, with sloping quarters and a straight shoulder. The legs are clean but in some cases can be sickle-hocked. Moreover, the placement of the pelvis tends to

BELOW & OPPOSITE: Despite its refined looks, the Don is extremely hardy and able to withstand the harsh climate of the Russian Steppes.

ABOVE, OPPOSITE & OVERLEAF: The Don was the preferred mount of the Russian Cossacks. Today thay are mainly used for riding and driving.

restrict movement and causes a stilted action – a fault that has now been largely bred out. The hooves are well-shaped and hard.

Tough and sturdy, with an independent spirit, these qualities have found their way into other breeds. The most striking feature of the Don's coat is its iridescent sheen. It is most commonly chestnut, but can also be bay, brown, black, and gray. It stands approximately 15.2hh.

DUTCH HEAVY DRAFT

The modern Dutch Draft is a relatively new breed, registered in the early 20th century when the Royal Association of the Netherlands Draft Horse was formed. However, documentation of a heavy draft horse has existed since around 1850, while Holland and Belgium have had heavy horses for centuries, most notably the Brabant and Ardennais, whose history is very ancient.

These horses were crucial to the prosperity of the farming community where their strength and massive feet made them capable of working heavy soil. It was these two breeds, along with native Zeeland-type mares,

The Dutch Draft has a large and square head, but also quite attractive with a flat forehead and small but gentle eyes. The ears are small and straight, the nose is straight, and the nostrils are large and flaring. The neck is short and well- developed, while the body is short and deep and massively strong. The legs resemble tree trunks with abundant feathering present on the legs.

It is agile for its size, with a lively gait. It has a long working life and is tough, intelligent, kind, willing, and immensely strong.

They are predominantly chestnut and bay, less commonly gray and black.

Their height is up to 17hh.

OPPOSITE, ABOVE & RIGHT: The Dutch Heavy Draft was popular with farmers, who used it for hauling heavy loads.

that created the Dutch Draft, the purity of which has long been protected with only registered parents allowed entry to the stud book.

The Dutch Draft is an enormous horse for its height and is still used for heavy work on farms and for pulling brewers' drays. It can also be seen in the show ring.

DUTCH WARMBLOOD

The Dutch Warmblood is a relatively new breed, its stud book having been opened in the Netherlands in 1958. It is enjoying huge success in showjumping and dressage and is in demand worldwide as a top-class competition horse.

The Dutch Warmblood differs from most European warmbloods in that it is not based on any breed which existed in slightly different form in previous centuries and which has been improved upon. It contains breeds from all over Europe. The bases of the Dutch Warmblood are the Gelderlander and the heavier Groningen, which have been in existence in the Netherlands since the Middle Ages. The breeds themselves consist of many European strains, the Gelderlander being a combination of Andalusian, Norman, Oldenburg, Hackney, and Thoroughbred, to name but a few. The Groningen was created from Friesian and Oldenburg stock, which was chosen to produce correct conformation, good paces and a strong presence. A kind and willing nature and a certain amount of hardiness were also valuable traits.

BELOW & OPPOSITE: The Dutch Warmblood one of the most celebrated of all the warmbloods. It excels in many disciplines.

FJORD

The Norwegian Fjord is most likely descended from the Przewalski or Asiatic Wild Horse, which in turn was descended from Ice Age horses. It seems to have retained many of its ancestors' characteristics, including the pale coat, the dorsal stripe down the back, and the occasional zebra stripes on the legs, which were typical of the ancient breed.

The primitive breed was improved over many hundreds of years by breeding with the Celtic Pony and Tarpan. The result has been utilized for thousands of years, and there is evidence of its use in raids and battles from Viking artifacts. The Vikings had a particularly bloodthirsty approach to selection: they allowed stallions to fight to the death, ensuring that the stronger specimens continued the breed.

Fjords still have their manes clipped in the manner seen on Viking rune stones; the mane is unusual in that the hair

BELOW & OPPOSITE: The Fjord is likely to be a descendant of the Przewalski or the Asiatic Wild Horse on account of its dorsal stripe which runs from its head to its tail.

is cream on the outer edges and black in the center, being a part of the dorsal stripe. The mane is therefore clipped so that the black part remains prominent.

The Fjord has been used to improve many other Northern European breeds, including the Icelandic and Highland. Today they can be seen over most of Scandinavia, mainly as children's riding ponies. The Fjord is sure-footed and excellent at trekking and long-distance endurance events. It is also popular in harness, where it has been successful in competition. Some are still used around the farm for light plowing and as packhorses.

The Fjord has an attractive head: it is short and wide with short, neat ears, a slightly dished face, and large nostrils. The eyes are large and kind, and the neck is short and thick, accentuated by the traditionally clipped mane. The body is sturdy, with sloping quarters and a low-set tail. The legs are strong with plenty of bone and the feet are tough and hard.

All Fjords are dun-colored, which is a body color that is a tan, gold or a related shade with darker (usually black or dark brown) points and primitive markings. White markings are discouraged, though a small star is acceptable. Some also have zebra stripes on the legs. The hooves are most often dark, but can be a lighter brown color on lighter-colored horses. Fjords stand between 13.2 and 14.2hh.

ABOVE & RIGHT: The Fjord's mane is usually clipped to reveal its distinctive dorsal stripe.

FRENCH TROTTER

The first race track used for trotting in France opened in Cherbourg in 1839, and the sport has never looked back since then. The first races were a means of selecting suitable stallions and became quite an event. The most popular trotters at that time were Norman and Anglo-Norman breeds; later, these were crossed with Norfolk Roadsters from Britain, and by the end of the 19th century the breed had been further enhanced by infusions of British Hackney, Orlov Trotter from Russia, and Thoroughbred. These breeds did much to create a popular and much respected trotter, and a later addition of American Standardbred seems to have completed the breed.

In 1906 a stud book was created for French Trotters, though the breed itself wasn't recognized as such until 1922. To be acceptable for registration it was necessary that the horse be able to trot .62 mile (1km) in 1 minute 42 seconds. This was later extended to include only horses whose parents had both been registered, thus ensuring the purity of the breed. Recently, however, even more infusions of Standardbred have been made to improve the breed and its paces; the result is a world-class trotting horse, said to be able to surpass the Standardbred itself. Although there

ABOVE & OPPOSITE: The French Trotter exudes quality and shows many characteristics of the Thoroughbred.

have been infusions of American Standardbred blood, the French Trotter has retained its unusual habit of trotting on the diagonal rather than adopting the lateral pacing of the Standardbred.

Today French Trotters are predominantly used in the sport for which they were bred, both under saddle and in harness; but they also make good riding horses and even jumpers. The horses that have been bred for riding have also been used to sire competition horses – the Selle Français in particular.

In appearance, the French Trotter's Thoroughbred ancestry is much in evidence in the noble head, broad forehead, medium-sized far-apart ears, and kind, intelligent eyes. The nostrils are large and flaring. The neck is long and well-developed, with a straight shoulder, deep chest, and well-formed, powerful quarters. The legs are muscular with plenty of bone and well-shaped hooves.

The French Trotter has all the fine characteristics of the Thoroughbred. It has a good turn of speed, plenty of stamina, and a kind and even temperament, though it is not without spirit. The harness horses are usually a little smaller and lighter than the ridden types. Like the Thoroughbred, all solid colors can be seen, with the occasional roan. Grays are quite rare. Trotters stand at around 16.2hh.

RIGHT: The French Trotter excels at both ridden and trotting races, and is known for its very well-balanced and level stride.

FRIESIAN

The Friesian is the Netherlands' only surviving indigenous breed. It is descended from a native breed that once roamed Friesland – the western part of the ancient region of Frisia – 3,000 years ago, and where the remains of a similar coldblooded horse have been found. As riding horses, the Friesian's history is an ancient one, with evidence that it was used by Roman soldiers when they were building Hadrian's Wall in around AD 150; this is supported by the fact that Fell and Dales breeds, native to the English Pennines, are also descended from Friesian stock. Friesian bloodlines are also present in the Orlov Trotter and in most American trotters.

Over the years, the original, rather heavy and plain breed was infused with Oriental and Andalusian blood; this improved the breed to such an extent that during the 17th

OPPOSITE & ABOVE: The Friesian is an ancient breed which has benefitted from oriental and Iberian blood. It is capable of performing classical dressage.

century, Friesians could be seen performing haute école alongside Spanish horses, and Friesians were in demand as elegant carriage horses. During the 19th century, however, the Friesian became something of a rarity, being almost exclusively restricted to Friesland, where it was used as a general riding horse and trotter. By the end of the First

GIDRÁN

The Gidrán was developed at the Mezöhegyes State Stud, which was founded by Habsburg Emperor Joseph II in 1785. This important breeding establishment in Hungary was also responsible for the development of the Nonius in the early 19th century and the Furioso from 1885. But in about 1816 it had developed another breed, the Hungarian Anglo-Arab or Gidrán. The Hungarians required a cavalry horse with the stamina, strength and courage of the Arab though rather larger.

The creation of the Gidrán was complicated as there is far more varied blood in its composition than the traditional Anglo-Arab with its varying amounts of Arab and Thoroughbred. The stud imported an Arab stallion said to have originated from the Siglavy (Seglawi) strain which was called Gidrán Senior. He was mated with various breeds of mare, such as Arab, Turkish, and Spanish-Naples. From these unions seven colts were born which became Mezöhegyes's premier stallions.

In 1820 the Spanish-Naples mare, Arrogante, gave birth to a colt which was named Gidrán II and became the foundation stallion of the breed; today all Gidráns

BELOW & OPPOSITE: The magnificent Gidrán has all the attributes of the Anglo-Arab, with enormous presence and elegance.

HAFLINGER

The history of the Haflinger is obscure and there are various opinions as to its true origins. It is thought to have come from the South Tyrol in Austria, close to its border with Italy; borders have changed many times throughout history, however, making the exact location impossible to pinpoint. The Haflinger is not unlike the slightly larger Italian Avelignese, and the two probably had common ancestors.

The Haflinger may have been the result of native stock breeding with Oriental horses, which were left behind when the Ostrogoths were driven north by the Byzantine forces in the 6th century AD. Another story is that King Louis IV of Germany gave a Burgundian stallion to his son as a wedding gift, which was mated with local mares of Oriental origin to produce the Haflinger breed; either way it would seem that Oriental bloodlines are present.

What is known for sure, however, is that the modern Haflinger breed was improved in 1868 when the Arab

BELOW, OPPOSITE: The attractive, versatile Haflinger is fast becoming popular in North America. The primary objective of the American Haflinger Society is to keep the breed pure.

OVERLEAF: A herd of Haflingers grazing in an idyllic, alpine meadow in the Dolomites, Italy.

stallion, El-Bedavi XXII, was imported to the region and bred with Haflinger mares; today, all Haflingers are related to this one stallion.

Today the Haflinger is still to be found in Austria, where it is closely monitored, not only in government-organized breeding programs but also by private individuals. The breed is popular the world over, particularly in Europe, where it is used in the forests and farms of the Tyrol. It is also useful in harness, and as a children's riding pony and family pet.

The Arab influence can be clearly seen in the Haflinger's fine head, which presents a sharp contrast to the

stocky body. The nose is slightly dished and the eyes are large and attentive. The ears are small and alert and the nostrils and muzzle neat. The neck is well-proportioned, with fine sloping shoulders, good withers, and a deep girth. The body is broad and strong, with muscular quarters and a high-set tail. Legs are of medium length with tough hooves.

The Haflinger has rhythmic, ground-covering gaits. The walk is relaxed but energetic, and the trot and canter are elastic, energetic, and athletic with a natural tendency to be light on the forehand and balanced. There is some knee action, and the canter has a very distinct motion forward and upward.

The Haflinger is a sociable animal and enjoys the company of people. It is intelligent, trustworthy and docile, making it an excellent work pony and safe with children. Haflingers are hardy and require only moderate feeding; but they do require shelter from cold winds and wet weather. Their most striking feature is their flaxen mane and tail that are usually left long.

Various shades of chestnut, liver, or red are permitted, sometimes with a little dappling over paler areas. It stands at a height of around 14hh.

BELOW & OPPOSITE: The Haflinger's head is rather refined, which is a consequence of its Arabian bloodlines.

HANOVERIAN

The German Hanoverian horse has a long history. The earliest reference to it as a warhorse was in the 8th century, when Charles Martel frustrated the advances of the Saracens at the Battle of Poitiers. These heavy warhorses were probably a mixture of native, Spanish, and Oriental influences.

Hanoverians owe their evolution to warfare, and by the Middle Ages had developed into large, cobby horses, capable of carrying a knight clad in full armor. The type was favored for many centuries until changes in warfare techniques meant that a lighter horse was eventually required. At this time, the Hanoverian was still a heavy

breed, even though it was somewhat taller and more agile than a cob; by the 17th century, three distinctive types were being bred for military purposes: Hanoverian, Mecklenburg, and Danish horses.

But it was in the 18th century that the Hanoverian truly came into its own, when a member of the House of Hanover, in the person of George I, ascended the British throne in 1714. He spent much of his reign in Hanover, however, and for the next 100 years or so the Hanoverian was nurtured and improved. English Thoroughbred

BELOW & OPPOSITE: The Hanoverian is known for its athleticism, beauty, grace, and good temperament.

ABOVE & RIGHT: The Hanoverian is one of the oldest and most successful of all the warmbloods.

stallions were bred with Hanoverian mares, and Cleveland Bay bloodlines were also added to produce a horse that was still relatively heavy but also suitable for farm use and coachwork.

It was George II who established the state stud at Celle in 1735, where horses for agriculture, riding, and driving were bred. Here the Hanoverian breed was improved still further, with additions of Trakehner and Thoroughbred blood; the Hanoverian breed registry was founded in 1888. This horse was very similar to today's famous competition horse.

HOLSTEIN

The German Holstein, or Holsteiner, is probably descended from a native breed known as the Marsh Horse, which once roamed the wetlands of the Elbe estuary in what is now Schleswig-Holstein. The Holstein breed dates to the 13th century, when Gerhard I, Count of Holstein and Storman, permitted the monks of the Uetersen monastery to graze their quality horses, which they bred themselves, on private land. These were native stock that had been mixed with

ABOVE & OPPOSITE: The Holstein is greatly respected as a sport horse, excelling in show jumping, dressage, and eventing.

By the 18th century the Holstein's reputation had become so great that vast numbers of horses were exported. Unfortunately, not all of them had been bred to the exacting standards that had once prevailed and general deterioration set in.

By the 19th century, fortunately, the decline had been halted, and measures were now being taken to save and improve the breed. As the demand for warhorses grew less, the Holstein came to be used as a quality carriage horse, and to this end, Yorkshire Coach Horses and Cleveland Bay stallions were mated with Holstein mares. This was a great success, and the breed was given a new lease of life.

Thoroughbred was also added to refine the breed after the Second World War, which also improved the Holstein's jumping ability and general character. Today, it is a supreme sporthorse, excelling at dressage, showjumping, and eventing. It has also been bred to good effect with other warmblood breeds, most effectively with the Hanoverian.

The Holstein is quite different from other warmbloods in that it has a large, rangy build resulting in a huge stride. The head is long and straight with large, flaring nostrils. The ears are expressive and the eyes are large and gentle. The long neck is elegant and well-developed, with high withers; the back is long and straight. The shoulders are shapely and sloping, which also contributes to its long stride. The chest is broad, the girth is deep, and the quarters are slightly sloping, muscular and powerful. The legs are long and muscular.

The Holstein is a fine, well-balanced horse, with an amazing ground-covering, elastic stride. The overall effect is of an elegant horse that carries itself lightly. It is good-natured, obedient and eager to work. Its large size and scope means that it is much in demand as a top-flight competition horse.

Holsteins are most commonly bay, though all solid colors, together with gray, are permitted. They stand around 16–17hh.

Icelandics have lately been exported to other countries, however, where cross-breeding has been allowed to take place.

This is a well-constructed animal. The head is of medium length, having a typical pony character with small pricked ears and soft, expressive eyes. The neck is well-set, and the chest is broad with a deep girth. The body and legs are stocky and strong and the feet are extremely hard.

The Icelandic is ideal for children, being tough, hardy and happy to live out all-year-round. It has two extra gaits: the *tölt*, which is a running walk with four beats, and is as fast as a canter and very comfortable; and the flying pace, which has two beats and is used for racing but which makes great demands on horse and rider. Speeds of up to 30mph (48km/h) can be reached using the flying pace, and to

witness this is impressive indeed. The Icelandic is late to mature, however, and should not be backed until it is four years old. It can live to a ripe old age, often working up until 30; in fact, an Icelandic in Britain is known to have died aged 42.

Icelandics come in all solid colors as well as skewbald, palomino, dun and gray. A silver dapple coat is much prized; this is where the body is a rich brown and the mane and tail appear almost silver by contrast. In winter the coat is very thick, with three distinct layers. Icelandics stand between 12 and 13.2hh, and have been known to reach 14.2hh.

BELOW, OPPOSITE & OVERLEAF: The Icelandic evolved from ponies brought to the island by Celts and Vikings in the 9th century.

KABARDIN

The Kabardin is descended from the Tarpan – the wild horse of Eastern Europe and Asia, which sadly became extinct in captivity in 1887. The Kabardin remained unchanged in type until the Russian Revolution when, like many other Russian horses, steps were taken to improve the breed. The original Kabardin was bred with Karabakh, Turkmene, Persian, and Arab to create a much bigger, stronger horse, suitable for riding and general farm work, also for use as a packhorse. The Kabardin is also an excellent mountain horse – possibly the best there is – being sure-footed, agile, and intelligent, with the innate ability to search out the safest routes. Its great stamina enables it to work all day without becoming stressed.

BELOW & OPPOSITE: The Kabardin is the principle breed of the Northern Caucasus and is used to improve native stock in Armenia, Azerbaijan, and Georgia. The best Kabardins are bred and raised at the Karachai and Malka studs.

These reconstituted Tarpans, as they are now known, live wild in a nature reserve where they are beginning to manifest many Tarpan characteristics. Today Koniks are mainly used for farm work and occasionally as children's ponies.

The Konik has strong head with great character that shows its Oriental origins. The neck is of medium length and quite thick but with a good carriage. The body is stout and sturdy with well-developed, medium-length legs, which are slightly feathered. The hooves are tough.

OPPOSITE & ABOVE: Koniks are kept in herds at various sites in Europe, including Poland, the Netherlands, and the UK. The breeding of the Konik in controlled conditions is vital to the breed's survival.

The Konik is hardy and will live out all year round with little extra feeding and care. Some can be wilful and difficult – a throwback to their wild Tarpan origins. Usually light-brown or dun and sometimes bay, the mane and tail are full and the dorsal stripe and zebra markings are sometimes visible. Height is 12.2–13.3hh.

LATVIAN

The Latvian is thought to have an ancient history, though no one can be certain of its origins; the general opinion is that it is either descended from the prehistoric Forest Horse, a heavy type that once roamed over northern Europe, or that it evolved from an indigenous Lithuanian pony crossed with Tarpan and Arab blood. It is thought that the latter is more likely.

Today there are three distinctive types of Latvian, depending on the other breeds with which it has become intermingled. The heaviest is the Latvian Draft which is the original breed present in the other two and which has

BELOW, OPPOSITE & OVERLEAF: The Latvian is a purpose-bred warmblood horse breed from Latvia.

been infused with Finnish Draft, Oldenburg, and Ardennes to make a substantial draft horse which is not so heavy that it cannot be ridden. The medium-sized version is the Latvian Harness Horse, which came into being in the 1920s when the original Latvian was bred with Hanoverian, Oldenburg, and Norfolk Roadster to make a lighter and more elegant carriage horse. The final, lighter, Latvian is a more recent addition, having received infusions of Arab and Thoroughbred to make a horse which is rather more of a warmblood and does well in competition. Today all three are still used by farmers and competition riders.

The three types may vary in stature, but they are all unmistakably Latvian. The head is longish and noble with a straight nose and large nostrils, proud eyes, and small well-shaped ears. The neck is long and nicely placed with sloping shoulders, a deep girth, and a longish body with well-developed quarters. The legs are shapely though volume of bone depends on type. The mane and tail are thick and full.

Latvians are incredibly strong with excellent stamina and an equable temperament.

They come in all solid colors and the occasional gray. Their height is 15.1–16hh.

LEFT: There are three types of Latvian: the Latvian Draft, the Latvian Harness Horse, and the Latvian Riding Horse. Today the lighter-weight Riding Horse is the most widespread, owing to the popularity of equestrian sports.

LIPIZZANER

The Lipizzaner is probably one of the world's most recognizable breeds due to its association with the Spanish Riding School of Vienna. Despite its origins in what is now Slovenia, the Lipizzaner has a far more ancient history, dating back to the 8th century and the Moorish occupation of Spain. The Moors brought horses of Oriental origin to Spain, such as Arabs and Barbs. These were bred with the heavier Iberian horses, which in turn produced the Andalusian – the most important element in the Lipizzaner's line of heredity.

In 1580 Archduke Charles, son of the Holy Roman Emperor Ferdinand I, who had inherited Austria-Hungary, sought to improve his horses and decided on the system of *haute école*, or the practice of advanced classical dressage. He founded a stud at Lipizza for the purpose, which also

BELOW & RIGHT: Lipizzaner stallions are trained in Haute école, *a form of classical dressage. The horses are based at the Spanish Riding School of Vienna but are transported all over the world to perform.*

OVERLEAF: Lipizzaners at stud.

LUSITANO

The Lusitano shares its heritage with the Andalusian, both having been descended from the Iberian riding horse. The Lusitano gets its name (adopted only in the early 20th century) from Lusitania, which was the Roman name for Portugal. The origins of the breed date to around 25,000 BC and to the ancient ancestors of the Sorraia pony, which can be seen in cave paintings throughout the Iberian Peninsula.

Unlike the Andalusian, the Lusitano's breeding has remained truer to its Sorraia ancestry, in that it has only received infusions of Oriental, Garrano, and Spanish blood. To keep the breed true to type, this mix hasn't been changed for centuries and care is taken to use only horses with obvious Iberian characteristics.

The Lusitano was bred mainly for agricultural use around the fertile river Tagus, where it is still used for that

sent to stud, and all fighting horses are left entire; it is believed that geldings lack the courage and intelligence to work in the bullring. Today, they are still used for farm work, bullfighting, and also for dressage. Infusions of Lusitano are also used to improve other breeds.

The Lusitano has a fine, noble countenance. The head is quite long, with a straight or slightly Roman nose and flared nostrils. The ears are of medium length, well-shaped, and alert. The eyes are keen and intelligent, the neck is set high, with a well-developed muscular crest and well-defined withers. The sloping shoulders are powerful and the chest is broad with a deep girth. The back is short and

OPPOSITE, ABOVE, RIGHT & OVERLEAF: The Lusitano has a shared heritage with the Andalusian of Spain, both being descended from Iberian stock, though the Lusitano has remained slightly truer to its origins.

purpose. It is also used in bullfighting, as well as in *haute école*. Thankfully, in Portugal, the bull is not killed, and the entire business takes place with the rider on the horse's back. However, the Lusitano has to be incredibly agile and fast to avoid injury.

These horses are highly prized and receive *haute école* training to enhance their precision so that they can survive the demanding and dangerous spectacle. The Lusitano stallions are trained to these high standards before they are

strong and the loins broad, with quarters that are not too large. The Lusitano's high-stepping action is attributed to its strong, long hocks, which are capable of great impulsion, and the deep flexion is achieved by a well-developed second thigh (stifle).

This noble and courageous horse is kind, good-natured and obedient. It is level-headed and not given to sudden panic, which are important attributes in a fighting horse.

Lusitanos have competed in several Olympics and World Equestrian Games as part of the Portuguese and Spanish dressage teams.

They may be any solid color as well as gray, and they stand between 15 and 16hh.

BELOW & OPPOSITE: Today the Lusitano is used in high-level competition and is particularly talented in dressage and driving.

MÉRENS

Ponies remarkably similar to the Mérens, and depicted in ancient cave paintings at Niaux, have roamed the Pyrenees of Andorra since prehistoric times. The native breed has changed slightly over the years with infusions from heavy horses arriving with the Romans and also Oriental bloodlines.

The Mérens has been used for plowing and hauling for hundreds of years by mountain farmers, where its stamina and sure-footedness make it suitable for the inhospitable terrain. The Mérens was also used for transporting lumber and also by soldiers in the Middle Ages and Napoleon during his campaigns.

The Mérens, or Ariègeois, is similar to the British Dales and Fell ponies and the Friesian. Breeders still raise their stock the traditional way: the ponies live out all year round and the foals are born in the spring snow. In the summer transhumance occurs when they are herded up high into the mountains where they are allowed their freedom for several months, after which time some are selected for breaking, selling on or breeding. Today they are still used for farming and forestry and also as children's ponies.

The Mérens is a most attractive pony, with a small, neat head, a slightly dished or straight nose, small pricked ears, and kind, soft eyes. The neck is short and well-developed, and the body strong and stocky with well-developed hindquarters. The legs are shortish with good bone and a little feathering around the fetlocks.

The Mérens is well-balanced, level-headed, and compliant, as well as energetic. It is tough and can withstand the harshest conditions.

Mérens are usually black with a thick mane and tail. There height is between 13–14.2hh.

RIGHT: The Mérens is kind and even-tempered, making it a good children's riding pony. It also works well in harness.

MURGESE

The Murgese comes from Apulia, the region of southeast Italy that extends into the "heel" of the peninsula and which is known as Puglia in Italian. The original breed is probably about 500 years old and is descended from native Italian breeds intermingled with Barb and later Thoroughbred.

In the 15th and 16th centuries the breed was used by the Italian cavalry. Over the centuries, however, the Murgese virtually died out, only to be revived in the 1920s; a stud book was opened in 1926. Today the Murgese is a rather inferior light draft horse which has no specific conformity.

The Murgese's head is rather plain but with a kind, honest expression. The general appearance is similar to that of the Irish Draft in stature, though the hindquarters tend to be weak with a low-set tail.

The Murgese has some jumping ability and is used as a general riding horse. It has a kind nature and is a willing worker.

They are usually chestnut, but gray or black are also possible. Their height is between 14–15hh.

BELOW & OPPOSITE: Murgeses are often ridden by the Italian mounted police.

NEW FOREST

The New Forest Pony is probably a descendant of the Celtic Pony, as are all the British native breeds, though the earliest mention of it was in the time of King Canute (c.995–1035), famous for ordering back the sea's incoming tide.

The New Forest is in the county of Hampshire in southern England and consists mainly of scrubland, bog and moorland, which has led to the development of a hardy animal, designed to survive harsh conditions. Over the years, Thoroughbred and Arab blood were introduced, mainly to increase size and performance and to improve the pony's appearance, but is was not until the end of the 19th century, during the reign of Queen Victoria, that a structured breeding program was initiated. At the same time, other British breeds were also introduced, such as Dartmoor, Exmoor, Welsh, Fell, Dales, and Highland ponies.

In 1891, the Society for the Improvement of New Forest Ponies was founded to ensure that there was an ample supply of quality stallions living in the New Forest and this, in turn, led to the official publication of the first stud book in 1910. Nowadays, although still living and breeding in their home environment, many quality ponies are also bred in private studs all over the world.

BELOW & OPPOSITE: The iconic New Forest pony is indigenous to the New Forest, Hampshire, England.

The New Forest Pony is one of the larger breeds native to Britain. It is an ideal child's or teenager's pony and excellent for driving. It has a well-proportioned body that is more slender than other British breeds, and well-formed feet.

The ponies are calm, good-natured and a pleasure to own – substantial enough for dressage, showjumping, and

ABOVE, OPPOSITE & OVERLEAF: The New Forest makes an excellent all-round competition and general riding pony.

cross-country; in fact, it is often said that a good New Forest Pony can rise to any occasion.

Coats can be any color, with touches of white, while height is in the range of 12–14.2hh.

Thoroughbred, Trakehner, Hanoverian, and Westphalian. Nowadays, the Oldenburg excels at dressage and showjumping; it retains its ability as a coach or carriage horse, however, and is used for the purpose to this day.

The Oldenburg is distinguished by its noble head and proud, workmanlike air. It has a high-set neck, long shoulder, strong back, and a well-muscled croup with strong joints. It can be used not only as an elegant dressage horse, but also as a powerful showjumper, having a large frame and a long, active stride.

The Oldenburg resembles a hunter type. Its character is equable, making it pleasant to handle and ride. It is usually black, bay, or brown, and stands between 16.2 and 17.2hh.

BELOW, OPPOSITE & OVERLEAF: Oldenburgs are born with elastic and expressive gaits, with a good deal of suspension. For this reason they are often used in dressage.

PERCHERON

The Percheron comes from La Perche in Normandy in northern France. The breed is an ancient one, dating back to 732, when Arab horses, abandoned by the Saracens after their defeat at the Battle of Poitiers, were allowed to breed with the local heavy mares of the region. The Percheron type was the result.

At this time, the horse was much lighter than its modern counterpart and was used for riding as well as for light draft work. The type remained popular until the Middle Ages and the Crusades, when Arab and Barb horses from the Holy Land were mated with Percherons. It was also around this time that the Comte de Perche brought back Spanish horses from his forays in Spain; these were also mated with the Percheron, with further infusions of Andalusian added at a later date.

By the 18th century, the original breed had become almost completely eradicated by additions of Thoroughbred and more Arab; in 1820 two gray Arab stallions were mated with Percheron mares, thus creating the predominantly gray color of the modern-day breed.

BELOW: The lighter-weight Percheron is suitable as a riding horse. This gray is competing in an advanced dressage competition.

OPPOSITE: The ancient breed of Percheron is well-known worldwide.

OPPOSITE & ABOVE: The Percheron is well-muscled, proud, and elegant. It is a willing worker and has great intelligence.

By now all the heaviness of the ancient breed had disappeared; consequently, heavy mares from other regions were bred with Percheron stallions to make them more suitable for agriculture and to formulate the breed as it is known today. The lighter Percheron still exists and is used as a heavy riding horse, while the heavy version is still used for farm and forestry work and, in some countries, for pulling drays. It is also popular in the show ring.

Over the years the Percheron has been heavily exported to other countries, such as the U.K., Canada, Australia, and other parts of Europe, which has helped in its recognization as one of the world's leading heavy breeds.

The Percheron's head is proud and elegant, for a heavy breed, with a straight nose, broad forehead, expressive eyes, and short, shapely ears. The neck is short to medium, well-developed and with great strength. The shoulders are nicely sloping and well-shaped, with a broad chest and a deep girth. The Percheron is fairly short in the back, which adds to its strength, with slightly sloping but broad quarters. The legs are short and sturdy, with well-shaped tough hooves with very little feather.

The Percheron possesses a good deal of elegance due to the large amounts of Arab blood that have been added over the centuries. It has an excellent temperament, is calm, obedient and easy to handle, and has a keen intelligence. It has a smooth but lively action which makes it comfortable to ride.

Mainly gray, Percherons can occasionally be black or dark chestnut. There are two types: the small Percheron, which stands between 14.1 and 16.1hh, and the large, which is somewhere between 16.1 and 17.3hh.

SHAGYA ARABIAN

The Shagya Arabian comes from Hungary's second most famous breeding establishment, the Babolna Stud, founded in the late 1700s; the other is the Mezöhegyes Stud.

In 1816 the military stipulated that all brood mares should be bred with Oriental stallions to provide cavalry and harness horses; stallions with mixed Oriental blood as well as Iberian crosses were also used. The results, although fairly lightweight, were horses that were tough and had a good deal of stamina.

Following this success, it was decided that the Bobolna Stud should concentrate on breeding horses with predominantly Arab blood, which was the beginning of the excellent Shagya Arabian.

Today's breed is descended from one Arab stallion, called Shagya, which was brought from Syria in 1836. He was fairly large for an Arab, standing at 15.2$^{1}/_{2}$hh, and was from the Siglavi or Seglawy strain. The stallion was typically Arab in conformation, with a fine dished nose, a proud high-crested neck, a short body, and a high-set tail. It was mated with the military-style mares to produce the first Shagya Arabians and subsequent breeding by selection has produced a beautiful, refined riding horse of the highest possible quality. Today Shagya Arabians make excellent

BELOW, OPPOSITE & OVERLEAF: The Shagya Arabian has a free and elastic movement like all Arabians. Slightly heavier than the Arabian, it is a popular choice for eventing, dressage, and endurance.

riding and competition horses and are also used for driving. They remain popular in their native land, but are relatively rare elsewhere.

The Shagya is very like the Arab in conformation, but a little heavier. The head is wedge-shaped, with a wide forehead and a straight or dished nose. The ears are neatly pointed and alert, and the eyes are kind. The muzzle is small and delicate, with large flaring nostrils. The neck is beautifully arched, well-muscled, and set high. The shoulders are sloping, with a broad chest and deep girth; the body is fairly short, with well-defined quarters and long, elegant legs; well-muscled at the top, the legs have more bone than those of the traditional Arab.

The Shagya has the constitution of the Arab but is bigger and stronger. It is kind, noble and spirited, and has great stamina, speed and agility.

All solid colors are acceptable, although many have inherited the Shagya stallion's gray color. Rarest of all is black. They stand somewhere between 14.2 and 15.2hh.

SHETLAND

The Shetlands consist of 100 or so offshore islands lying off the north-eastern coast of Scotland. The islands are remote and have a harsh climate, particularly in winter, and there is not much shelter for the ponies that inhabit them. Food is scarce, but the ponies have adapted to survive on very little. They live on next to nothing during the winter months, but it is known that they come down from the hills to feed on the seaweed that has been washed up on the beaches.

It is unclear where these ponies originated, but there is evidence from Bronze Age remains that they have been present for a very long time, probably descended from the Celtic Pony. Alternatively, they may have crossed the ice from Scandinavia, or may even have come from Europe.

Traditionally, Shetlands were used by islanders as riding, plowing, pack and harness ponies. In 1870, the Londonderry Stud at Bressay, Scotland, fixed the type and character of the breed and today's best stock can still be traced to the famous Londonderry sires, even though the stud no longer exists.

BELOW, OPPOSITE & OVERLEAF: The Shetland is an ancient breed dating back 2,500 years. Today it is mainly used as a child's pony.

The Shetland's head is small and neat and can be slightly dished. The ears are small and the eyes open and bold. The neck, shoulders and withers are well-defined; the chest and quarters must be strong and muscular. The mane and tail is profuse, with straight feathering on the legs. The coat is double-layered – a feature unique to the Shetland Pony.

The Shetland has plenty of character and can be willful on occasions. Because it is relatively strong for its size, unless it has been properly trained and has good manners, it may be too much for a small child. But when kept in a suitable environment, with adult help on hand, Shetlands make superb children's ponies.

Shetlands can be most colors, and black, brown, bay, chestnut, gray, piebald, and skewbald are all common.

Standard Shetlands grow to a maximum height of 42in (107cm). Since the 1980s, however, a miniature Shetland has been developed which does not exceed 34in (86cm).

SHIRE

The English Shire is one of the most famous and distinctive of all the draft horses and one of the largest and most majestic breeds in the world. Descended from medieval warhorses, whose immense strength enabled them to carry knights into battle wearing full armor, it was probably based on the Friesian horse, with later infusions of Brabant. It was brought to England by the Dutch to drain the fens of East Anglia, but it was not until the late 19th century that the best heavy horses in England were selected to develop the breed as it is known today.

The Shire's strength also made it suitable for agriculture and heavy haulage work, so initially the breed was established in Lincolnshire and Cambridgeshire, where strong horses were required to cope with heavy fenland soil; but the Shire soon became widespread in Staffordshire, Leicestershire and Derbyshire, until it eventually spread over England as a whole.

Up until the 1930s, the Shire was widely seen across the country, but numbers dropped dramatically when mechanization of farming began to appear, putting the breed in danger of disappearing altogether. Fortunately, the

BELOW & OPPOSITE: The majestic Shire is the largest and strongest horse breed in the world.

problem was detected by a few dedicated breeders who helped to promote the breed and restore it to its former glory.

The Shire Horse Society has worked tirelessly to raise funds and encourage the spread of the breed to other countries. Today, there are active Shire Horse societies across Europe, the United States, Canada, and Australia. Although a few Shires are still used on farms today, they are kept mainly for the sheer pleasure of working them in their traditional roles. They are also used in plowing competitions, again, for pleasure, and for the same reason are used in pairs by breweries to deliver beer locally; the spectacle obviously makes for excellent publicity.

The Shire's most significant feature is its sheer size and massive muscular conformation. It is the largest and strongest horse in the world and weighs a ton or more when mature. Built ultimately for strength, the chest is wide, the back short-coupled, the loins and quarters massive. The legs, joints and feet are sufficiently large to balance and support the Shire's weight; the lower legs are covered with long, straight, silky feathers. In the show ring, white feathers are generally preferred as they help to accentuate the horse's action. Even though the Shire is such a large horse, it is not an ungainly heavyweight; in fact it is very much in proportion and quite awesome to behold. The head is always noble, the nose slightly Roman, and the eyes are large and wise.

The Shire is well-known for its patient, gentle and placid nature; it is a true "gentle giant." In fact, it is quite amazing that such a strong animal weighing so much can be so easily handled, and it is not uncommon to see them ridden or handled by children or small women. Its kindness is legendary.

Black, brown and gray are the recognized colors of the breed. White feathers on the legs are preferred for the show ring, and white face markings are common. They stand somewhere between 16.2 and 18hh.

LEFT: Despite its large size, the Shire is surprisingly agile.

SUFFOLK PUNCH

The Suffolk Horse, usually known as the Suffolk Punch, originated in East Anglia in England. It takes its name from the county of Suffolk, while "punch" is an old word meaning "short and thickset." It is thought to date back to 1506 and is the oldest heavy breed in Britain.

The breed was first developed by crossing the native heavy mares of the region with imported French Norman stallions. Modern-day Suffolks, however, can be traced back on the male side to a single, nameless stallion, foaled in 1768 and belonging to Thomas Crisp of Orford, near Woodbridge, Suffolk. Even though the breed is relatively pure, infusions of Norfolk Trotter, Thoroughbred, and Cob were added during the centuries that followed.

Immensely strong, it is also quite agile, due to its relatively small size. These qualities, combined with a lack of feather on the legs, like the Percheron, made it ideal for working the heavy clay soils of East Anglia. Moreover,

LEFT, ABOVE & OPPOSITE: The Suffolk Punch is Britain's oldest breed. Sadly it is now very rare.

its economical food consumption, in proportion to its size, enabled it to work for long days on the farm without stopping.

As with many of the heavy breeds, numbers fell dangerously low when farm tractors became widespread. Today, Suffolks are rare, even though there has been a concerted effort to increase numbers in recent years. Today, Suffolks are shown, used in plowing competitions, or are kept by breweries for their novelty value.

The Suffolk Punch is always chestnut in color (the traditional spelling in this instance is chesnut, without the "t"). The breed is well-known for its great strength, and its extremely powerful, muscular body, with relatively short legs, provides a low center of gravity; this enables the horse to pull plows or vehicles that much more easily.

Suffolks mature early and can do light work when they are 2 years old. They continue working well into their 20s.

The Suffolk is docile and hardworking. It is capable of almost any kind of work and is easy to maintain. Height is between 16.1 and 17.1hh.

SWISS WARMBLOOD

The Swiss Warmblood is based on Switzerland's highly respected Einsiedler breed which dates back at least to the 11th century; in fact, there is evidence that Benedictine monks in Einsiedeln were breeding the horses as early as 1064.

For many centuries the Einsiedler, which is strong and athletic, was used as a riding and driving horse. Gradually the breed was enhanced when Norman and Hackney blood were added and a little later infusions of Anglo-Norman were also introduced.

ABOVE & OPPOSITE: The Swiss Warmblood is a quality horse which excels in competition.

But it was in the 20th century that the breed really took off when Selle Français and Anglo-Arab were added, making the horse much finer and warmblooded. Then in the 1960s the Swiss decided that they wanted their own performance and competition horse, so using the remodeled Einsiedler they introduced other European warmbloods such as Hanoverian, Holstein, Trakehner and Thoroughbred.

The result was the Swiss Warmblood, a high-quality sports horse that excels at dressage, showjumping, and carriage-driving competitions. In its early stages, the National Stud at Avenches used imported stallions, but now that the breed has developed its own standard Swiss Warmbloods are used.

They have a head is of medium size and good quality with a straight or slightly dished nose, intelligent eyes, and alert medium-length ears. The neck is long and elegant with a slight crest. The body is of medium length with a good strong sloping shoulder, broad chest, and deep girth. The legs are long and well developed with well-shaped hooves.

These quality horses are known for their excellent paces and superb jumping ability, having had many successes in international competition. They are kind, willing, and easy to train.

They may be all colors and stand around 16hh.

RIGHT: The Swiss Warmblood has been bred for its excellent paces, making it the perfect dressage horse.

The Tersky is a horse of medium height and great beauty, which reflects its Arabian heritage. The head is finely formed with a dished profile; the eyes are large and intelligent and the nostrils flared.

The Tersky has an equable temperament that combines kindness and intelligence with courage and stamina.

They are predominantly gray, usually with a metallic sheen to the coat, while black, chestnut, and bay are also possible. They stand between 15 and 16hh.

ABOVE & OPPOSITE: The Tersky is an excellent sport horse thanks to its Arabian heritage. It is refined and fine-coated but can still cope well in a harsh climate.

Although initially bred with racing in mind, the qualities of the Thoroughbred make it an ideal horse for all other equestrian disciplines, e.g. eventing, showjumping, dressage, etc. Not only has the Thoroughbred been exported far and wide to improve racing stocks, it has also been used to improve hundreds of other breeds around the world.

Descendants of the three foundation sires reached the United States in the 1730s, where they were generally similar to Thoroughbreds elsewhere; recently, however, a distinctive American type has emerged, with longer hindlegs and a longer stride, making its quarters appear higher in comparison.

The Thoroughbred is a beautiful and athletic animal, with long, clean limbs, a fine, silky coat, an elegant profile, and a muscular body. The eyes are always large and intelligent and the ears finely sculpted. Built for toughness, stamina and speed, the Thoroughbred is regarded as the ultimate racing machine.

Thoroughbreds are courageous, honest, and bold, and one only has to be present at a steeplechase or hurdle race to see that this is so. The Thoroughbred is often described as "hot-headed," and while this may be true of some individuals, which are more sensitive than others, most are a pleasure to own and ride.

Pure-bred and Thoroughbred are not synonymous in this context: the latter, in this case, is the actual name of this breed.

All true colors are acceptable, and height is usually between 15 and 16.2hh.

BELOW, OPPOSITE & OVERLEAF: Thoroughbreds are bred for speed and endurance, rather than temperament, so they can be spirited.

VLADIMIR HEAVY DRAFT

The Vladimir originated at the turn of the 20th century in the provinces of Vladimir and Ivanovo to the north-east of Moscow.

Local mares were mated with imported heavy breeds, mainly Clydesdales, but were also crossed with Shire, Cleveland Bay, Suffolk Punch, Ardennais, and Percheron. The result is a horse suitable for all heavy draft work.

The breed was officially recognized in 1946 and from then on only horses which satisfied strict conformation criteria and performance tests were registered.

A horse that matures early, the Vladimir Heavy Draft can be put to work and stud when it is 3 years old.

The Vladimir has all the hallmarks of a heavy breed, with a muscular body, broad chest and strong neck. Its legs are sturdy and well-muscled.

The breed is remarkable for its proud posture and majestic appearance. Unlike some of the other heavy breeds, its paces are forward-going, making it suitable for pulling troikas. Today, the Vladimir is still used for work on farms and in transportation. They are mainly bay, black and chestnut and stand at 15.2–16.1hh.

BELOW, OPPOSITE & OVERLEAF: The Vladimir Heavy Draft has all the fine attributes of a heavy horse, with an alert and proud bearing and lively attitude.

THE WELSH BREEDS

Horses were present in Wales as much as 10,000 years ago. At that time, the indigenous breed inhabiting the hills was the Celtic Pony, and it is thought that all Welsh ponies known today derive from this ancient breed.

It is recorded that native stock was being bred in Wales in around 50 BC, when Julius Caesar founded a stud in Merionethshire and was responsible for introducing Arab blood into the breed. The first mention of Welsh ponies and cobs appears in the laws of Hywel Dda, written in AD 930.

Throughout the centuries, variations on the original wild ponies were developed. Early on in the 20th century, the Welsh Pony and Cob Society identified the four clear types. These are the original, once wild, Welsh Mountain Pony not exceeding 12hh (Section A); the Welsh Pony not exceeding 13hh (Section B); the Welsh Pony of Cob Type up to 13.2hh (Section C); the Welsh Cob of 13.2–15.2hh (Section D).

The Welsh Mountain Pony (Section A) is the oldest of all the Welsh breeds. As the name suggests it is tough, resilient,

BELOW: The Welsh Mountain Pony (Section A) is the oldest of the Welsh pony breeds.

ABOVE: The Welsh Pony (Section B) has refined looks combined with strength and toughness. It is an excellent choice for a children's riding pony.

sound in limb as well as constitution. Known for its intelligence, agility, endurance, and hardiness, the Welsh Mountain Pony is capable of surviving the harshest of winters. These ponies are now found all over the world and are highly regarded as quality children's riding ponies; they also perform well in harness.

The head is refined, with a slim tapering muzzle and small, pricked ears. The eyes are large and bold. These qualities, as well as a dished face, give the Welsh Mountain a distinct resemblance to the Arab, a breed that has been introduced. The neck, well-defined withers and quarters are in proportion to the rest of the pony's body, while the tail is set quite high. The limbs are set square, with well-made joints, and the feet are small, rounded and hard.

The Welsh Mountain has great personality and charm, having inherited intelligence and quick-wittedness – traits which the original wild ponies seemed to have possessed in abundance. When in action, the gaits should be smooth and the hocks well-flexed. They are usually gray, but all true colors are acceptable.

LEFT: A Welsh Section B.

OPPOSITE & ABOVE: The Welsh Pony (Section C) should resemble a small cob in appearance. It is used for riding and driving.

The Welsh Pony (Section B) has all the best attributes of the Welsh Mountain Pony, though breeders have accentuated its talents as a riding pony. Moreover, because the Welsh Pony has been used for generations on farms for herding sheep, it has similar toughness and agility.

These qualities, when combined with good looks, jumping ability, and superb conformation for riding, makes them perfect as children's mounts.

The Welsh Pony shares many similarities with the Welsh Mountain Pony. The head is refined, with small pricked ears, and the face may be slightly dished. The eyes are large

and intelligent. The neck, back, and quarters are muscular and in proportion, and the tail is set high. The limbs are straight and strong and the hooves strong and rounded.

The Welsh Pony is willing, active and enthusiastic and will always give of its best. Like the Welsh Mountain they are predominantly gray, but all true colors are acceptable.

The Welsh Pony of Cob Type (Section C) was originally used for farm work – also for carting slate from the mines. It is of a similar height to the Welsh Pony, but sturdier and capable of carrying heavier loads. It was developed more as a harness pony than for ridden work and has a naturally pronounced action, probably inherited from the Hackney, which was introduced into the breed.

General appearance is of a small cob. The eyes are spaced widely apart and the expression is intelligent. Like the others, the ears are small and pricked. The body and

legs are sturdier and more cob-like than those of the Welsh Pony, and the feet are slightly larger. Mane and tail are full.

The Welsh Pony of Cob Type is similar in temperament to the other Welsh breeds, being lively and enthusiastic. It performs well in harness and is also a natural jumper.

All true colors are acceptable, but for the show ring, ponies are preferred with plenty of white on the lower legs.

Of all the Welsh breeds, the Welsh Cob (Section D) is the most famous. Known for its handsome appearance and extravagant paces, not only is it the ultimate working cob, it is also guaranteed to command attention in the show ring.

The breed dates from the 11th century, when it was known as the Powys Cob or Powys Rouncy. Welsh Cobs not only possess Welsh Mountain Pony blood, they were also influenced by imports from all over the Roman Empire. Breeds from Spain, such as the Andalusian, and the Barb, and Arab from North Africa, were all crossed with the early Welsh Cob variety. Later in the 18th and 19th centuries other breeds, such as Hackney and Yorkshire Coach Horse, were also introduced.

Welsh Cobs were traditionally used by the military as well as by farmers, but they were so versatile that they could be used by virtually anyone needing transport or light haulage.

The Welsh Cob is compact, well-muscled, well-balanced, and strong. It has a fine head with large, intelligent eyes, and the usual small, pricked ears. The neck is arched and muscular, the back is short-coupled for strength, and the quarters are powerful and rounded. The legs are sturdy and straight and the hard and rounded feet are in proportion with the animal's body.

The Welsh Cob is proud, courageous, and extravagant in action. It is suitable for all disciplines and for all riders.

All true colors are acceptable.

LEFT: The Welsh Cob (Section D) is cobby in appearance. It is larger than the other three types and is most attractive with extravagant paces. Its size means that it can be ridden by adults as well as children.

WESTPHALIAN

Like most European warmbloods, the Westphalian is based
on an older, heavier breed which had been native to
Westphalia for hundreds of years. This native coldblood
was crossed with Thoroughbred to produce a warmblood,
which was first registered as a Westphalian in 1826, when
the stud book was opened.

For many years, the horse was used for riding and light
carriage work until measures were taken to improve the
breed at the end of the Second World War. To improve its
speed and endurance, as well as its intelligence,
Westphalian stock was infused with more Thoroughbred
and Arab blood, while Hanoverian was also added to
ensure good sense and obedience.

The result was a riding horse of superb quality which
received its true recognition as a competition horse,
particularly in showjumping, in the 1970s. Nowadays it not
only excels at dressage but also at eventing.

The head is handsome and broad, with medium- to
wide-apart ears, a straight nose, and clever eyes. The neck
is long and well-developed, with fairly prominent withers,
a straight back, strong loins, and well-muscled quarters.
The shoulders are sloping, with a broad chest and deep
girth. The legs are well-porportioned and strong with
plenty of bone.

The Westaphalian is well-known for its courage and
spirit. It is also obedient and easy to handle.

All solid colors are permitted, with white on the lower
legs and head, and a height between 15.2 and 16.2hh.

*LEFT: The Westphalian is another German success story, originally
bred as a carriage and riding horse. However, it now excels at dressage,
eventing, and showjumping.*

CHAPTER SEVEN
HORSES OF ASIA

"The wind of heaven is that which blows between a horse's ears."

—Arabian Proverb

AKHAL-TEKE

The Akhal-Teke of Turkmenistan, a republic in central Asia lying between the Caspian Sea and Afghanistan, is believed to be a descendant of the Turkoman or Turkmene, an ancient race of horses thought to have existed thousands of years ago, but now unfortunately extinct. It takes its name from the Teke tribe, which still inhabits the Akhal Oasis in the Karakum Desert, close to the border with Iran. Here the horses are traditionally kept in herds under the watchful eyes of mounted herdsmen. This aristocrat of the desert is

LEFT, ABOVE & OPPOSITE: The Akhal-Teke is famous for the iridescent sheen to the coat in some individuals.

long, slim elegance personified, but it also has a hardy constitution and can go for long periods without water. In their protected environment, however, the horses are well-tended by the herdsman, who use heavy rugs to cover their backs during extremes of heat and cold. They were once hand-fed a high-protein diet, which surprisingly included eggs and mutton fat.

Historically, this "heavenly" horse was prized by such warlords as Alexander the Great, Darius the Mede, and Genghis Khan, while Marco Polo praised the Turkoman

horse in his *Travels*. Nowadays, because of their great agility and athleticism, Akhal-Tekes are most often used for racing and in endurance events.

The Akhal-Teke appears to break almost every rule of good conformation. Its head is carried high on a long, thin neck set at an angle of 45 degrees to the body, giving it a proud, slightly haughty appearance. It has a fine, elegant head with wide cheeks and a straight or slightly dished nose; the large eyes are bold and expressive. The nostrils are dry and flared and the ears shapely and alert. Although the shoulders are broad and sloping, the chest is quite narrow. The body is fairly short, rounded and shallow, and the long loins have little definition. The girth is quite narrow, and the very long legs appear disproportionately long in relation to the body, and taper to small hooves.

It has an unusually smooth-flowing and powerful action. The shape of the pasterns are unique to the breed, possibly developed from negotiating desert terrain.

The Akhal-Teke is not known for its sunny nature, in fact, quite the reverse. It is willful and rebellious and benefits from one firm handler which it can learn to trust. It is an intelligent animal which requires careful and sympathetic training; it does not respond well to punishment and may very well retaliate. Due to its genetic inheritance it is unlikely to flourish cooped up in a stable and must be allowed a predominantly outdoor life, with plenty of space to wander.

Colors may be chestnut, bay, gray, palomino, black, and dun. All the colors, apart from raven black, are strikingly iridescent. Height is approximately 15.2hh, though, with its pronounced withers and high head-carriage, the horse appears taller.

RIGHT: The Akhal-Teke is a proud breed, with a reputation for speed and endurance.

ARABIAN

The Arabian (Arab) is one of the oldest of the hotblooded breeds, and its bloodlines are present in many modern horses found throughout Europe and the United States. The name is not strictly accurate, as the original "Arab" may well have been a small Oriental-type wild horse, living in Eastern Europe, the Near East and the Middle East. The Arab was further developed as Islam assimilated the breed, and Muslim invaders used it as a cavalry horse. Today's modern Arabians can trace their descent from five foundation mares, known as Al-Khamesh (The Five), said to have been selected for their obedience.

The Arab was also of great importance to the Bedouin, the nomadic tribe of the desert, which can trace its association with the breed to 3000 BC, to the mare Baz and the stallion Hoshaba.

OPPOSITE & ABOVE: Bedouin breeders of the past carefully recorded bloodlines and jealously guarded the purity of their horses. As a result, today's Arabians are as immediately recognizable as ever.

Arab horses were so-named when they were imported from the Arabian Peninsula to Britain in the 19th century. The Arab is also the foundation of the Thoroughbred. Arab blood is therefore highly effective when mixed with other breeds, and usually brings great improvements to any offspring that result.

Arabs are extremely beautiful, with a delicacy that belies their strength and stamina. They shine in riding events, such as dressage, riding horse, and in-hand showing. They also excel in disciplines that rely on strength, such as endurance riding and racing. Arabs have the reputation of being unable to jump, which is quite untrue; they are keen jumpers, but lack the ability to compete at high level.

The head is short and refined, with a dish-shaped profile and a tapered muzzle with large nostrils. The eyes are large, wide-apart, and low-set, and the ears are small, shapely and set well apart. The jaw is rounded and forms a curved arch where head and neck meet, known as the *mitbah*.

The back is slightly concave, with sloping shoulders and well-defined withers. The croup is level and the girth deep. The tail is set high. The legs are strong, hard, and clean, with flat knees, short cannons, and well-defined tendons; the hooves are hard and tough. The Arab also has a distinctive skeletal feature, in that it has fewer vertebrae, i.e. 5 lumbar, 17 rib and 16 tail, compared with 6-18-18 in other breeds, giving it a short-coupled appearance.

The horse's action is as if it were floating on air. Due to their desert origins, Arabs have fine coats and skin which is designed to release heat. Consequently, they require special care in winter, though they are tougher than Thoroughbreds.

Arabs are famous for their intelligence, loyalty, and responsiveness. They are also affectionate and respectful of other animals, also of human beings, being especially good with children. The reverse side of their character is that they are fiery and courageous; they can also be stubborn if asked to do something against their will.

All solid colors are possible, but chestnut and gray are the most common. Arabs usually stand somewhere between 14 and 15.2hh.

BELOW & OPPOSITE: The Arabian is an ancient breed whose blood has been used to improve many other breeds. It was of primary importance in the development of the Thoroughbred.

MARWARI

The Marwari, from the Marwar region of Rajasthan, India, is similar in appearance to the Kathiawari, but is of much greater stature; it has often been featured in Indian art over the centuries. The Marwari is unusual in that it has a fifth gait, called the *revaal*, which is a long, smooth action with little vertical movement, which makes it very comfortable to ride.

Marwari numbers declined during the British occupancy of India, but thanks to today's Rajput families, and others interested in the continuation of the breed, the Marwari is once again flourishing. It is now used as a

OPPOSITE, ABOVE & OVERLEAF: The Marwari was once a great warhorse and has featured in Indian art for centuries. Thanks to renewed interest the breed is once more gaining in popularity.

dancing horse, popular at weddings and festivals. Its dance is a form of *haute école*, which the horse would have been taught when it was a warhorse long ago.

It has a high, proud head-carriage with a straight or Roman nose, its trademark ears curving inward until they almost meet in the center. The eyes are large, bright, and intelligent; the neck is of medium length and arches in movement. The coat is fine and silky.

The Marwari has a naturally flamboyant presence and loves to perform, but it is also tough and able to survive harsh conditions. It is courageous, intelligent, and a willing worker.

Marwaris may be any color, including roan, piebald, and skewbald. They stand between 15 and 16hh.

PRZEWALSKI'S HORSE

This is a truly ancient breed, also known as the Mongolian or Asiatic Wild Horse. Primitive horses of this kind were hunted by man 20,000 years ago and the likenesses of similar horses can be seen in prehistoric cave paintings in Spain and France. The breed was almost certainly extinct in the wild, but recent introductions of herds has led to a new population. Genetically, it is the only true wild equine and the distant ancestor of the domestic horse.

ABOVE, OPPOSITE & OVERLEAF: The wild Przewalski's Horse cannot be domesticated, tamed, or ridden.

The earliest written evidence of its existence was in the 9th century, and it was mentioned again in 1226, when a herd of wild horses are supposed to have caused Ghengis Khan, the founder of the Mongol Empire, to fall from his horse.

Because of its isolation and the fierceness with which stallions protect their mares, the Mongolian horse's bloodline has remained pure and can be traced back to its primitive ancestors.

It gets its modern name from the man who brought it to the attention of the world, Colonel N. M. Przewalski, a Polish explorer who acquired the remains of a wild horse in 1881 from hunters who had discovered them in the Gobi Desert. He took them to the zoological museum in St. Petersburg, where naturalist I. S. Poliakoff examined them and decided that they belonged to a species of primitive wild horse. Following the discovery, some of the living horses were caught and kept in captivity in zoos and wildlife parks so that they would be saved from total extinction.

The captive population has increased rapidly and is carefully monitored at Prague Zoo, which holds the stud book of the breed. The horses are kept in conditions that are as natural as possible; some have been released back into the wild in China, Russia, and Mongolia, where they are a protected species, and a successful population can also be found in France.

The Przewalski is stocky and has an erect, dark-brown mane. The head is of medium size, with a broad forehead and a straight or slightly dished nose. The wild-looking eyes are set high on the head and are rather small. The nose tapers to a narrow muzzle with small, low-set nostrils. The body is strong, with a longish, straight back, a thick, short neck, and weak quarters. The legs are short and stocky with hard, tough hooves.

Przewalskis cannot be tamed and tend to be aggressive and ferocious, especially in the presence of their young. Being extremely hardy, they need very little extra attention.

Various shades of dun, ranging from yellow to red, are possible. Przewalskis have black manes and tails and black legs, often with zebra markings, and there is a black dorsal stripe running down the back. The muzzle and the area around the eyes is a creamy-white color. They range in height from 12–14hh.

CHAPTER EIGHT
HORSES OF AUSTRALIA & AFRICA

"Horses lend us the wings we lack."

—Anonymous

AUSTRALIAN STOCK HORSE

The Australian Stock Horse, otherwise known as the Waler, has a history that began in the 18th century, when horses were imported into Australia from South Africa and Chile. These tended to have excellent constitutions, being descended not only from Iberian, Arab, Barb, Criollo, and Basuto stock, but also from Indonesian ponies. The quality of the first horses was found wanting, however, but later infusions of Arab and Thoroughbred brought great improvements to the stock.

The breed, also known as the New South Wales Horse, was once important as a cavalry horse. It was used by the British in India from about 1850, but soon became popular with stockmen, who saw its soundness and endurance as distinct assets in the huge expanses of the Australian outback; it was also used in harness.

BELOW, OPPOSITE & OVERLEAF: The Australian Stock Horse today is still predominantly used by stockmen, where its hardiness and stamina are assets on the enormous sheep and cattle stations in Australia.

By the 1940s, the Waler, as it was now generally known, had become a quality horse, but after the Second World War the population was allowed to dwindle. It was also bred with other horses, which subsequently weakened the breed. Today, steps are being taken to improve the Waler by adding Quarter Horse, Arab, and Thoroughbred, but it has yet to be regarded as a consistent breed.

The ideal Waler has a fine head with a broad forehead, straight nose, and medium-length alert ears. The eyes are kind but inquisitive and intelligent. The neck is long and elegant with a slight crest, and the shoulders are sloping.

The chest is broad with a deep girth, while the body is of medium length with strong loins and well-developed quarters. The legs are strong with shapely hooves.

The Waler has many excellent qualities. It is obedient and willing to work and is kind and intelligent. They are most often bays, though all solid colors are possible. They stand between 15 and 16.2hh.

BELOW & OPPOSITE: The Australian Stock Horse is also used for trail riding vacations in the Australian outback.

BARB

The Barb has ancient origins, its name having been taken from a location in North Africa, once the fabled Barbary Coast, a section of the Mediterranean littoral stretching from Morocco to Egypt. Here, 2,000 years ago, cavalry horses were bred by Hannibal's Carthaginian forces.

At an early stage, the breed was probably influenced by the Arabian horse, brought to North Africa by the Arabs – also by hotblooded Oriental types. A great many were

imported to Europe, particularly England, where many references to "Barbary" horses are to be found, the most famous being Richard II's "Roan Barbary." Here they were also bred for the cavalry and were prized for their speed and great stamina. Today it is difficult to find a pure-bred Barb. This is because of the widespread cross-breeding practised throughout the Mahgreb, its purpose being to produce good general riding horses.

The Barb is not a handsome horse and is inclined to be bad-tempered, but it has had a tremendous influence on other breeds, particularly in Europe and the Americas. The Andalusian of Spain, the Connemara Pony of Ireland, the Thoroughbred, and even the Criollo of South America are all believed to have Barb blood running through their veins.

Today the Barb is used for general riding, racing, and display purposes. It remains very popular in its native land but receives little recognition elsewhere.

The Barb, bred for desert life, is fairly lightweight. The head is long and narrow, with a slightly dished face and medium well-shaped pointed ears; the eyes are kind and intelligent. The neck is of medium length, with a pronounced crest. The withers are prominent and the shoulders flat. The legs are fine, but strong, and the hooves are hard and well-shaped – a feature of all desert horses. The mane and tail are full, with the tail set low on flat quarters.

The Barb is quite stand-offish and inclined to be irritable, but it has a reputation for extreme toughness, speed and stamina – qualities which have made it suitable for improving other breeds.

Most common colors are black, bay, and dark brown, though Barbs with Arab blood may have coats of other colors, such as gray. The height range is 14.2–15.2hh.

LEFT & OPPOSITE: The Barb is prized for its stamina and endurance. Pictured here are Barb horses in traditional Moroccan tack.

OVERLEAF: These horses are taking part in the traditional Fantasia Horse Show in Morocco. The horses in the show are of Arabian, Andalusian, or Barb stock.

BASUTO

The Basuto, or Basotho Pony, is from Lesotho, previously Basutoland – an enclave of South Africa. The Basuto, bred mainly by the Bantu, was a development of the Cape Horse in the 19th century. By the early 20th century the breed had virtually disappeared, due to indiscriminate crossings with Thoroughbred, Indonesian and Spanish horses in an effort to produce more substance.

The Basuto was eventually saved by a society established to improve and revive the breed in the later 20th century. In addition to the usual walk, trot and canter, the Basuto has two extra gaits, known as the triple and the pace.

The head is rather large, with an underdeveloped, shortish neck. The body and legs are strong and wiry, with hard hooves. Recent breeding programs have improved the Basuto, however, and the neck is now more shapely and the head finer.

The Basuto is tough and can survive adverse conditions on very little food and water. It is sure-footed, fast and fearless. It is only used for riding, as all draft work in Lesotho is done by cattle.

They come in all colors, as well as gray, and their height is usually around 14.1hh.

LEFT: A Basuto pony having a well-earned rest in front of Maletsunyane Falls in the mountainous highlands of Semonkong, Lesotho, Africa.

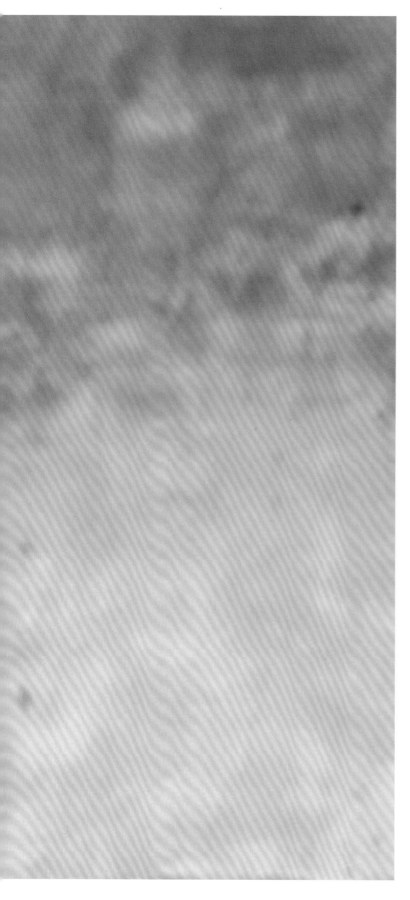

BOERPERD

The Boerperd or Boer Horse, has a history that runs side by side with the white settlers of South Africa and the arrival of the Dutch in Cape Town in 1652.

The first horses seen in the region were of Oriental blood and were imported from Java, which in turn were sold by the Dutch East India Company to the Free Burghers in 1665. Over the years, however, significant inbreeding had taken place and measures were taken to improve the breed by introducing Arabian blood to the stock.

This practice continued for 150 years until a definite type emerged, known as the Cape Horse. Meanwhile, some Iberian breeds arrived in the Cape in 1793, which may or may not have had an effect on the native horses. In the late 18th and early 19th centuries, Cape Horses remained very popular and were prized for their endurance, stamina, speed, and intelligence, which made them useful in a military role.

Over the years, various other influences affected the breed, and Flemish horses, Hackneys, Norfolk Trotters, and Cleveland Bays brought further improvements. The breed continued to survive, despite disease and the Boer Wars, in which the horses certainly proved their worth.

The Boerperd (Afrikaans for farm horse) owes much of its appearance to its Oriental and Arab forebears. The head is small and wedge-shaped, with a slightly dished or straight nose, and it has a small, neat muzzle with flared nostrils. The eyes are bright and intelligent and the ears are medium-sized and alert. The body is short and compact, with a neatly sloping shoulder, deep girth, and well-proportioned muscular legs with plenty of bone. The hooves are tough and shapely.

The Boerperd is spirited, courageous, and intelligent, with plenty of stamina and agility. They come in most solid colors and gray, and range from 14.2–15.2hh in height.

LEFT & OVERLEAF: The Boerperd took its name from the Boer Wars in which it was widely used.

BRUMBY

Australia had no native horses of its own until they were introduced during the country's gradual colonization, and in particular by settlers, who arrived during the 19th-century gold rush. Not only was there an influx of people, therefore, but also a large intake of horses and other animals.

During the First World War, many of the horses escaped or were turned loose to run wild: these were the forefathers of the modern-day Brumby, a name said to have been derived from the aboriginal word for "wild" (*baroomby*).

Because of the variety of animals that reverted to a wild state, there is no specific breed type; consequently Brumbies come in all shapes, sizes and colors.

The horses are now almost totally feral, making them difficult to catch and almost impossible to train. They are prolific breeders and for this reason, in the past, have come to be regarded as pests. This has led to such extensive culling that they are now quite rare. They come in all colors and patterns. Height is up to 15hh.

ABOVE & OPPOSITE: Australia has no native breeds of her own; the Brumby was introduced by settlers who turned their horses loose and let them run wild.

460

Acknowledgements

All photographs in this book are under license with

©Shutterstock.com

The copyright holder wishes to stress most emphatically that persons engaging in the sport of riding must not do so without the protection of officially approved headgear.